# HITLER'S MILITARY HEADQUARTERS
## Organization, Structures, Security and Personnel

by
Aaron L. Johnson

## 1st Edition ~ 1999

Copyright 1999 by Aaron L. Johnson

Published by R. James Bender Publishing,
  P.O. Box 23456, San Jose, California 95153
  Phone: (408) 225-5777
  Fax: (408) 225-4739

Printed in the United States of America

ISBN No. 0-912138-80-7

# Table of Contents

# Foreword

This work covers the various headquarters from which Hitler conducted the German military effort during the Second World War. It also details all of his movements during the course of the war. Based on a book published by Druffel Verlag in Germany *(Das Führerhauptquartiere 1939-1945: Zeitgeschichte im Bild),* numerous photographs have been added from various archives as well as considerable unpublished material concerning the composition of Hitler's headquarters, its guards, plus its higher military and political staffs.

Hitler's first wartime headquarters was his *Führersonderzug* which transported him to a number of temporary locations during the Polish campaign. In preparation for the offensive against France, headquarters commander General Rommel and members of his staff were sent west to look for a suitable headquarters location. Near Bad Nauheim they decided on Ziegenberg castle which they updated and added protective bunkers. This installation was called *"Adlerhorst"* (Eagle's Nest). Hitler felt this *FHQu* was too luxurious, however, as he valued his reputation as a leader with only modest personal comforts. A new installation was built near Wiesental, just a short distance away. It should be noted that Hitler did not use *"Adlerhorst"* until the Ardennes Offensive in December 1944.

A suitable location was then chosen at Rodert near Münstereifel which was 65 kilometers south-west of Bonn and 45 kilometers from the Belgian border, and became known as *"Felsennest"* (Cliff Nest). This simple installation was used during the initial phases of the French campaign in May 1940. As the German forces pushed forward, Hitler wanted to move his *FHQu* westward. On May 22 a new site at Brûly-de-Pesche was chosen, which was just south-west of Couvin in Belgium, and was called *"Waldwiese"* (Forest Meadow). When Hitler occupied the modest location on June 6 he renamed his headquarters *"Wolfsschlucht"* (Wolf's Gorge). A second installation was later prepared in 1943-44 near Margival, France. It was well built and had a nearby tunnel which could house the *Führer-sonderzug* and was named *"Wolfsschlucht II."* It was not used until the invasion of Normandy by the Allies. The *Führer* only spent one day there on June 17, 1944 to meet with his field commanders.

The next *FHQu* was located in the Black Forest near Freudenstadt and was given the name *"Tannenberg"* (Pine Mountain). This served as Hitler's base of operations during his excursions to Strasbourg in the Alsace and to some World War I battlefields.

Hitler returned to Berlin on July 6, 1940 and all *FHQu* units were transferred to the *"Adlerhorst"* location. After usage, *"Felsennest"* was turned over to a guard company of VI Military District Command and *"Wolfs-schlucht"* to *Organisation Todt. "Felsennest"* was utilized once more during Hitler's Christmas visit to the troops in December 1940.

Because the offensive against Yugoslavia in April 1941 had not been planned in advance, no special headquarters had been established. Therefore, the *Führersonderzug* had to be utilized. A length of railroad track outside of a tunnel near Mönichkirchen, south of Wiener Neustadt, was chosen as the temporary *FHQu*. Here, the locomotive which was constantly ready, could pull into the tunnel immediately if necessary. This location was known as *"Frühlingssturm"* (Spring Storm).

With military preparations for the invasion of Russia, a new *FHQu* was being established just east of Rastenburg in East Prussia, and was known as *"Wolfsschanze"* (Wolf's Lair). Hitler took up residence at his new headquarters on June 24, 1941, and spent a considerable amount of time there until November 20, 1944 when the Red Army was getting dangerously close. During this time he made a number of extended trips to Berlin and Munich at his residence, the *"Berghof,"* for state affairs. From July 16 to October 30, 1942, and February 17 to March 13, 1943 he moved to a more forward headquarters just north of Vinnytsa in the Ukraine, at an installation called *"Wehrwolf."* Here he could more closely observe the activities of Army Group South.

There were three inner security zones inside *"Wolfsschanze"* and they were known as Hitler's *Sperrkreis I* (Restricted Zone I), *Sperrkreis II* and *Sperrkreis III*. The situation on the Eastern Front was becoming critical by late November 1944. Hitler had left *"Wolfsschanze"* on November 20 and by November 22 Field Marshal Keitel made sure all preparations had been made so that the *FHQu* would be destroyed before falling into Soviet hands. The code-name for this operation was *"Inselsprung"* and by mid-January 1945 the *"Wolfsschanze"* bunkers were blown up.

As mentioned earlier, Hitler finally went by rail to Giessen and then by car to the *"Adlerhorst"* installation during the Ardennes Offensive in December 1944. On January 15, 1945 he returned to Berlin and conducted operations from the Reichs Chancellery until the end.

After the war the occupying forces and their subservient German government officials went to great lengths to physically destroy as many of Hitler's homes and headquarters as they could, but some of these still survive in various forms of decay.

Aside from some limited coverage, there has been very little written about Hitler's military headquarters which were scattered on both fronts in Europe. It is hoped, therefore, that this work will be of some service to both historians and researchers.

~ Aaron L. Johnson

# Publisher's Acknowledgements

During the research and production of this book the following individuals and institutions were generous with their time, efforts, and archives, with the sole purpose of making it a more complete and accurate work. My personal thanks go to them.

Ian M. Baxter
Stan Cook
Hoover Institution, Stanford University
Bohumir Kudlička
Jess Lukens
National Archives
George A. Petersen
Otto Spronk

# Hitler's Military Headquarters Staff, 1941-1945

## Oberbefehlshaber der Wehrmacht

1. *Der Führer und Oberste Befehlshaber der Wehrmacht,* **Adolf Hitler.**

**Adolf Hitler**

2. *Chefadjutant der Wehrmacht beim Führer und Obersten Befehlshaber der Wehrmacht* (also *Chef des Heerespersonalamtes*) until 1st October, 1944: *Generalmajor* (1st April, 1943 *Generalleutnant,* 27th July, 1944 *General der Infanterie*), **Rudolf Schmundt,** born 13th August, 1896, 1914 *Fahnenjunker,* 1915 *Leutnant in Füsilier Regiment 35; Reichswehr* 1931 *Hauptmann;* 1935 *Major;* 1936, *Staff,* 18th Division; 28th January, 1938, *Chef Adjutant der Wehrmacht beim*

*Führer;* 1st October, 1938, *Oberstleutnant;* 1st January, 1942, *Generalmajor,* simultaneously *Chef Heerespersonalamt* in October of 1942; 1st April 1943, *Generalleutnant;* 20th July, 1944, seriously wounded by assassination attempt at *FHQu;* died on 1st October, 1944 in military hospital at Rastenberg.

Schmundt is shown standing behind Hitler in his command vehicle. Erich Kempka is driving.

Rudolf Schmundt

Wilhelm Burgdorf

From 12th October, 1944: *Generalleutnant* (1st November, 1944 *General der Infanterie),* **Wilhelm Burgdorf,** born 15th February, 1895, 1st August, 1914, *Fahnenjunker;* 18th April, 1915, *Leutnant Grenadier Regiment 12; Reichswehr, Major* and Tactical Instructor *Dresden Kriegsschule;* 1st October, 1937, Adjutant, IX Army Corps;

1st August, 1938, *Oberstleutnant;* 30th April, 1940 until 4th April, 1942, Commander Infantry Regiment 529; *Oberst,* 1st September, 1940; 1st May, 1942, Head of Section 2 in *Heerespersonalamt; Generalmajor* 1st October, 1942; 1st October, 1942, Acting Chief of the *Heerespersonalamt;* 1st October, 1943, *Generalleutnant;* 1st October, 1944, *Chief Heerespersonalamt;* 1st November, 1944, *General der Infanterie.* Vanished from *Führerbunker* 2nd May, 1945. Believed to have worked for US intelligence after 1945; *Ritterkreuz.*

3. *Adjutant der Wehrmacht (Heer) beim Führer und Obersten Befehlshaber der Wehrmacht* from 10th March, 1938 through 1st October, 1943, *(Hauptmann,* from 1st January, 1940 *Major,* 1st February, 1943 *Oberstleutnant),* **Gerhard Engel,** born 13th April, 1906. *Fahnenjunker,* 5th October, 1925; 1st September, 1930, Leutnant, Infantry Regiment 5; 1st March, 1937; *Adjutant des Heeres beim Führer und Reichskanzler;* 1st October, 1943, Infantry Regiment 27; 1st May, 1944, Oberst; 28th June, 1944, 12th Infantry Division; 1st November, 1944, *Generalmajor;* 1st April, 1945, *Generalleutnant;* 12th April, 1945, Division "Ulrich von Hutten;" *Ritterkreuz mit Eichenlaub.*

Gerhard Engel

Hitler and Engel at the Berghof.

From 26th September through 22nd October, 1943 through the end of March, 1945 *Major (Oberstleutnant* from 1st January, 1944) **Heinrich Borgmann,** born 15th August, 1912. *Leutnant,* 1935; *Hauptmann,* 1940 and CO 3rd Battalion, Infantry Regiment 46; End of 1942 *Major* with the 3rd *Luftwaffe* Field Division; January, 1943 Staff Officer with 327th Infantry Division, June 1943, Operations Officer, 94th Infantry Division; 26th September,1943, seconded to the *Adjutantur der Wehrmacht;* 22nd October, 1943, Adjutant. End of March, 1945, CO of a *Fahnenjunker* Division; Killed in action April of 1945. *Ritterkreuz mit Eichenlaub.*

National Archives

Borgmann assists Hitler in awarding Oakleaves to the Knight's Cross on June 20, 1944. From left to right: Bernhard Flachs, Fritz Müller, Ernst Wilhelm Hoffmann, Wolf Hagemann, Gottfried Weber, Friedrich Hochbaum, Ludwig Müller and Ernst Eberhard Hell.

National Archives

Heinrich Borgmann

Acting from 21st July through 24th October, 1944, *Oberstleutnant* **Erik von Amsberg,** born 21st October, 1908. 1932, *Leutnant,* Cavalry Regiment 14 as Regimental Adjutant in 1936 and Squadron Leader in 1938; September, 1939 with *General Kommando XI* Army Corps; May, 1940, Adjutant to the Chief of the OKW; June, 1941, CO Reconnaissance Unit 46; April, 1942, *Major; OKH;* April, 1944, Staff Officer for Cavalry Matters on the Staff of the OKH; April, 1944, *Oberstleutnant;* 21st July, 1944 seconded to the *Adjutantur der Wehrmacht beim Führer;* end of October, 1944, Adjutant *AOK* 19.

From April, 1945, *Major* **Willy Johannmeyer** (see 6).

Fritz Darges, Erik von Amsberg, Walter Hewel and Hans Pfeiffer.

4.  *Adjutant der Wehrmacht (Kriegsmarine) beim Führer und Obersten Befehlshaber der Wehrmacht* from September, 1939 *Kapitän zur See* **Karl-Jesko von Puttkamer,** born 24th March, 1900. 1917 Naval Cadet; 1921, *Leutnant zur See;* 1930, *Kapitänleutnant;* 1935, Naval Adjutant to the *Führer;* 1936, *Korvettenkapitän;* September, 1938, Commander destroyer *"Hans Lody;"* August through September, 1939, Naval Liaison Officer to the *Führerhauptquartier;* October, 1939 through April, 1945, Naval Adjutant to the *Führer* und *Obersten Befehlshaber der Wehrmacht;* November, 1939, *Fregattenkapitän;* 1st September, 1943, *Konteradmiral.*

5.  *Adjutant der Wehrmacht (Luftwaffe) beim Führer und Obersten Befehlshaber der Wehrmacht* from 1937 through April 1945, *Major* **Nicolaus von Below,** born 20th September, 1907. 1929, *Reichswehr,* Infantry Regiment 12; 1933, joined the *Luftwaffe;* 1935

Von Puttkamer looks on as Hitler presents Grand Admiral Dönitz with his baton.

Karl-Jesko
von Puttkamer

*Fliegertruppe Döberitz;* 1936 *Staffelkapitän* in Fighter Squadron 134 *"Horst Wessel;"* 1937, *Hauptmann* and Adjutant of the *Wehrmacht* to the *Führer;* 1941, *Major;* 1st March, 1943 *Oberstleutnant;* 1st March, 1944, *Oberst.*

Nicolaus von Below

13

6. *Offizier in der Adjutantur der Wehrmacht* from November, 1944 through April, 1945 *Major* **Willi Johannmeyer,** born 27th July, 1915. 1938, *Leutnant* Infantry Regiment 64; 1942, *Hauptmann;* 1943, CO 2nd Battalion, Grenadier Regiment 503; end of 1943, Major; November, 1944, *Heerespersonalamt* and *Adjutantur der Wehrmacht beim Führer;* April 1945, replaced Borgmann as Army Adjutant; *Ritterkreuz mit Eichenlaub.*

Willi Johannmeyer

Fritz Darges

7. *Persönliche Adjutanten des Führers* from March, 1942 through March, 1943, *SS-Sturmbannführer* **Fritz Darges,** born 8th February, 1913. 1933, SS; 1934, *Junkerschule Tölz;* 1935, *Untersturmführer 2. Standarte SS-VT;* 1936 through 1939, Adjutant to Bormann; 1937, *Obersturmführer;* 1940, *Hauptsturmführer,* Battalion Adjutant and Company Leader in West campaign; October, 1940, *Persönliche Adjutant der Führer;* March 1942 through March 1943; January,1943, *Sturmbannführer;* August, 1944, *Abteilung* Commander and later CO of the Panzer Regiment in the 5th SS Panzer Division *"Wiking." Ritterkreuz.*

*SS-Hauptsturmführer* **Richard Schulze-Kossens,** born 2nd October, 1914. 1934, *Leibstandarte SS "Adolf Hitler;"* 1935, *SS-Junkerschule Tölz;* 1936, *Untersturmführer;* Autumn 1938, Adjutant to the Chief of the *SS Hauptamt* and *NAPOLA;* April, 1939, Adjutant to von Ribbentrop, Foreign Minister; January, 1941, *LSSAH;* 1941, Hitler's *Ordonnanzoffizier;* 29th October, 1942, *Persönliche Adjutant des Führers;* 22nd February, 1943, *Sturmbannführer;* 15th November, 1943 Tactical Instructor and Training Group Commander at the *SS-Junkerschule Tölz;* 25th July, 1944, again *Persönliche Adjutant des Führers;* January, 1945, *SS-Junkerschule Tölz.*

Hitler and Schulze-Kossens.

Richard Schulze-Kossens

*SS-Hauptsturmführer* **Hans Pfeiffer,** born 5th December, 1912. 1933, SS Panzer Training; 1937, *Untersturmführer;* 1939 as *Oberersturmführer, Ordonnanzoffizier* with Hitler's SS Escort Command; January, 1942, *Hauptsturmführer;* August, 1942, Staff Officer for the 1st SS-Panzer Division; October, 1942, *Persönliche Adjutant des Führers;* 10th June, 1944 as Company Leader in the

Hans Pfeiffer

12th SS Panzer Division *"Hitlerjugend"* killed in action. Posthumous promotion to *Sturmbannführer.*

*SS-Untersturmführer* **Otto Günsche**, born 24th September, 1917. 1934, *LSSAH;* 1936, *Unterführer* in Hitler's SS Escort Command; June, 1942, *Untersturmführer* following a course at the *SS-Junkerschule* and a tour of front line duty; January through August, 1943, acting *Persönliche Adjutant des Führers;* August, 1943, 20th April 1943, *Obersturmführer;* Company Chief, 1st Battalion, SS Panzer Division *"LAH;"* February, 1944 until 10th April, 1945, *Persönliche Adjutant des Führers;* 20th April, 1944, *Hauptsturmführer;* 21st December, 1944, *Sturmbannführer.*

Linge is at far left as Hitler presents the Oakleaves to *Generalleutnant* Werner Ziegler and *Leutnant* Gerhard Hein on September 23, 1942.

8. *Ordonnanzoffizier des Führers, SS-Hauptsturmführer* **Heinz Kersten,** born 28th November, 1920. 1938, SS, *"LSSAH;"* Campaign in Poland with *"LSSAH;"* 1941, *Untersturmführer* SS Division *"Wiking;"* 1942, Platoon and Company Leader 1st SS Division *"LAH;"* October, 1944, *Führerbegleitkompanie;* November 1944, *Hauptsturmführer;* 2nd December, 1944 became *Ordonnanzoffizier* at the *FHQ.*

9. *Hitler's personal servant* (valet), *SS-Obersturmführer* **Heinz Linge,** born 28th November, 1920. 1933, SS; 1935, personal body servant of Hitler; 1939, *Untersturmführer* in Hitler's Escort; 1942, *Obersturmführer;* 20th April, 1944, *Hauptsturmführer;* 24th February, 1945, *Obersturmbannführer.*

Otto Günsche        Heinz Linge

# Oberkommando der Wehrmacht

10. *Chef des Oberkommandos der Wehrmacht, Generalfeldmarschall* **Wilhelm Keitel,** born 22nd September, 1882. 18th August, 1902, *Leutnant* Field Artillery Regiment 46; 1920, Tactical Instructor at the Cavalry School; 1922, Chief 7th Section; Artillery Regiment 6; 1924, *Major;* 1925, Army Organization Department in the *Reichswehrministerium;* 1927, Section Commander, Artillery Regiment 6; 1929, *Oberstleutnant* and Chief of the Army Organization Department in the *RWM;* 1st October, 1931, *Oberst;* 1st April, 1934, *Generalmajor;* 1st October, 1934, *Kommandant* of Bremen; 1st October, 1935, Head of the *Wehrmachtsamt* in the *RKM;* 1st January, 1936, *Generalleutnant;* 1st August, 1937, *General der Artillerie;* 4th February, 1938, Chief, *Oberkommando der*

**Wilhelm Keitel**

*Wehrmacht;* 19th June, 1940, *Generalfeldmarschall;* Executed at Nuremberg 16th October, 1946; *Ritterkreuz.*

11. Adjutant *(Heer)* to the *Chef OKW, Hauptmann* **Ernst John von Freyend,** born 25th March, 1909. 1936, *Leutnant der Reserve* in Artillery Regiment 28; 1937, Active Duty; 1941, *Hauptmann;* February, 1942, *OKW/WZ;* 15th March, 1942, *Heeresadjutant beim Chef OKW;* 1st April, 1943, *Major.*

Schltze-Kossens, von Amsberg, Hitler and von Freyend (far right) who was wounded in the July 20 bomb attempt.

12. *Chef des Wehrmachtführungsstab im OKW, General der Artillerie* **Alfred Jodl,** born 10th May, 1890. 28th October, 1912, *Leutnant* in Bavarian 4th Field Artillery Regiment; 1921, *Hauptmann;* 1931, Major; 1932, *Reichswehrministerium;* 1933, *Oberstleutnant;* 1935, *Oberst* and Chief of the National Defense Section of the *RWM;* 1st October, 1938, Commander Artillery Command 44 in Vienna; 26th August, 1938, *OKW/Chef Wehrmachtsführungsamt;* 19th July, 1940. *General der Artillerie* (advanced past the grade of *General-leutnant);* 30th January, 1944, *Generaloberst;* executed at Nuremberg, 16th October, 1946; *Ritterkreuz mit Eichenlaub.*

Alfred Jodl

13. *Generalstabsoffizier beim Chef WFSt* from 25th August through 31st October, 1943, *Oberstleutnant* **Eckhard Christian,** born 1st December, 1907. 1926, *Reichsmarine;* 1930, *Leutnant zur See;* 1934, *Oberleutnant* in the *Luftwaffe,* Reconnaissance Flight School (Naval), *Warnemuende;* 1935, *Hauptmann;* 1938, *Luftwaffe* General Staff; 1939, Adjutant to the Chief of the General Staff of the *Luftwaffe;* March, 1940, Operations Officer, *Xth Flieger Korps;* June. 1940, *Major* and Group Commander in *Kampfgeschwader 26;* January, 1941, *Wehrmachtsführungsstab;* 1942, *Oberstleutnant;* 1st April, 1943, *Oberst;* 25th August, 1943 Chief of Staff of the *Luftwaffenführungsstab;* September, 1944, *Generalmajor* and Chief of the *Luftwaffenführungsstab;* 22nd April, 1945, Chief of the Liaison Staff of the *Chefs des Generalstabes der Luftwaffe zum OKW/Stab Nord.*

1st November, 1943 through 28th February, 1945 *Major* **Heinz Waizenegger,** born 22nd October, 1913. 1932, *Landespolizei;* 1939 *Lieutenant* of Police; 1935, transferred to the Army as Adjutant to the 3rd Battalion, Infantry Regiment 56; 1937, *Oberleutnant;* 1938, Chief 9th Company Infantry Regiment 56; 1940, *Hauptmann, General Kommando,* 5th Army Corps; March, 1942, transferred to *Panzer AOK 3;* 17th August, 1942, General Staff officer in the *Wehrmachtsführungsstab;* May, 1943, *Major;* March, 1945, Chief of Staff of *AOK 2.*

From 1st March, 1945, *Major* **Hermann Brudermueller,** born 22nd July, 1914. 1935, *Leutnant* Artillery Regiment 15; 1938, *Oberleutnant;* 1939, Regimental Adjutant, Artillery Regiment 51; 1940, 129th Infantry Division; 1941, *Hauptmann;* 1942, transferred to 110 Infantry Division and to the *General Kommando XXIII* Army Corps; November, 1942, 122 Infantry Division; June, 1943, *Major;* August, 1943 *OKW/WFSt* (Operational Section); 20th April, 1945, *Oberstleutnant.*

14. *Generalstabsoffizier beim Chef WFSt* (Adjutant to the Chief of the WFSt) until 31st October, 1943, *Major* **Heinz Waizenegger** (see 13).

From 1st November, 1943, *Major* **Herbert Büchs,** born 20th November, 1913. 1937, *Leutnant;* 1940, Staff of *Luftwaffe* Bomber Squadron 77; December, 1941, Air Force War Academy; October, 1942, *Hauptmann* on the staff of *Luftwaffen Kommando Don;* March, 1943, *VIII Flieger Korps;* August 1943, *Major* in *Luftwaffenführungsstab;* November, 1943, *WFSt.*

15. *Stellvetretender Chef des Wehrmachtführungsstabes* until 5th September, 1944, *Generalleutnant* **Walter Warlimont,** born 3rd October, 1894. 1914 *Leutnant* Foot Artillery Regiment 10; *Reichswehr* 1925, *Hauptmann* in the *RWM;* 1929, seconded to the United States Army; 1933, *Major* in the *RWM;* 1935, *Oberstleutnant;* 1936, CO of the 2nd Section, Artillery Regiment 34; 1937, CO Artillery Regiment 26; 1938, *Oberst;* October, 1938 Head of National Defense Section of the *OKW;* November, 1938, until September 1st, 1939, Acting Chief of the *Wehrmacht-führungsamt;* 1940, *Generalmajor;* January, 1942, Acting Chief of the *WFSt;* April, 1942, *Generalleutnant;* 1st April, 1944, *General der Artillerie;* October, 1948, sentenced to life imprisonment at Nuremberg; released in 1954.

From 15th November, 1944, *Generalleutnant* **August Winter,** born 18th January, 1897. 1917, *Leutnant* in the 2nd Bavarian Telegraph

Walter Warlimont                    August Winter

Battalion; 1933, *Hauptmann;* 1934, *Kriegsakademie;* 1936, *Major;*
1937, *OKH;* 1939, *Oberstleutnant;* October, 1940, Operations
Officer, Army Group A; April, 1941, Army Group South; July,
1942, Army Group B; 1941, *Oberst;* April, 1943, Chief of the
General Staff of the 2nd *Panzer* Army; August, 1943, *Generalmajor*
and Chief of the General Staff of Army Group F; August, 1944,
*Generalleutnant;* 30th October, 1944, transferred to the *OKW/WFSt;*
15th November, 1944, Acting Chief of the *WFSt;* 20th April, 1945,
*General der Gebirgstruppen.*

16. 1. *Generalstabsoffizier Heer im WFSt* until August, 1944, *Oberst* **Horst
Freiherr Treusch von Buttlar-Brandenfels,** born 2nd September,
1900. 1918, *Leutnant* in Hussar Regiment 10; 1933, *Rittmeister;*
January, 1937, *Major;* December, 1937, *Generalstab des Heeres;*
1939, *Oberstleutnant* and Chief of Staff, 81st Infantry Division;
1940, Operations Officer, Group XXI Norway, later *AOK*
Norwegen;12th January, 1942, 1st General Staff Officer, Army in
the *WFSt;* February, 1942, *Oberst;* 1st January, 1944 *Generalmajor;*
15th November, 1944, *Führerreserve;* January, 1945, transferred to
the *Ob.* West for assignment as Divisional commander; April, 1945,
CO 11th Panzer Division.

From 20th August, 1944, *Oberstleutnant* **Wilhelm Meyer-Detring,**
born 9th May, 1906. 1928, *Leutnant* Infantry Regiment 7; 1936,
*Hauptmann;* 11938, IX Army Corps; 1939, Quartermaster IX Army
Corps; February 1940, Operations Officer, 229th Infantry Division;

July, 1940, *Major* on the Staff of the *Wehrmacht* Command with the *Reichsprotektor*, Bohemia-Moravia; October, 1940, Operations Officer 137th Infantry Division; 1942, *Oberstleutnant* and Staff officer Army Group D; 1st September, 1944, *Oberst*.

17. 1. *Admiralstabsoffizier im WFSt* until 24th August, 1943 and acting from 4th November, 1944, *Fregattenkapitän* **Wolfe Junge**, born 5th January, 1903. 1926, *Leutnant zur See;* 1934, *Kapitänleutnant;* 1936, Watch Officer *Panzerschiff "Admiral Graf Spee;"* 1937, *Korvettenkapitän* and *Marineakademie* posting; 1938, *Referant im OKM;* April, 1939, Group Leader in *WFSt;* 1941, *Fregattenkapitän;* 1st April, 1943, *Kapitän zur See;* 25th August, 1943, First Officer Battleship *"Tirpitz"* (1st May, 1944 Commander of *"Tirpitz;"*) 4th November, 1944, again with the WFSt; 11th January, 1945, *Erster Führungsstabsoffizier Marineoberkommando Ostsee.*

From 25th August, 1943, *Kapitän zur See* **Heinz Assmann**, born 15th August, 1904. 1926, *Leutnant zur See;* 1934, *Kapitänleutnant;* 1937, *Referant im OKM;* October, *Marineakademie* posting; 1938, *Korvettenkapitän* und *Admiralstabsoffizier beim Marinegruppenkommando Ost;* November, 1939, *Referant im OKM;* between January and March, 1941, representative of the *SKL* with Admiral Lütjens on the Battleship *"Gneisenau;"* April, 1942, *Fregattenkäptain;* September, 1942, First Officer of the Battleship *"Tirpitz;"* June 1943, *Kapitän zur See;* 25th August, 1943, *WFSt.*

The First General Staff Officer of the *Luftwaffe* in the *WFSt*, *Oberst* **Berg** and *Oberstleutnant* **Böhm-Tettelbach**, did not take part in the military conferences because the General Staff officers of the Army and *Luftwaffe* with the Chief of the *WFSt* performed these functions.

18. *Chef des Heeresstabes beim Chef OKW und* (from 15th January, 1945), *Chef der Wehrmachtrüstung Generalleutnant* **Walter Buhle**, born 26th October, 1894. *Leutnant*, Infantry Regiment 124; 1926, *Hauptmann* in the *RWM;* 1930, Company Chief, Infantry Regiment 13; 1932, *RWM;* 1933, *Major;* 1936, *Oberstleutnant* and CO 2nd Battalion, Infantry Regiment 87; 1937, Operations Officer, *General Kommando,* Vth Army Corps; December, 1938, Chief, 2nd Section, Army General Staff, 1939, *Oberst;* 1940, *Generalmajor;* January 1942, Chief of the Army Staff with the *OKW;* April, 1942, *Generalleutnant;* 15th January, 1944, *General der Infanterie.*

19. *Beauftragter des Führers für die militärische Geschichtsschribung, Oberst* **Walter Scherff**, born 1st November, 1898. 1917, *Leutnant,*

Walter Buhle                    Walter Scherff

*Fusilier* Regiment 122; 1920, Infantry Regiment 13; 1929, Staff, 5th Division; 1931, *Kommandantur* Berlin; 1932, *RWM;* 1933, *Hauptmann;* 1935, Army General Staff; 1936, *Major;* 1937, Staff of 21st Division; 1938, Army General Staff; 1939, *Oberstleutnant OKH/AHA;* February, 1940, Staff, Commander the Reserve Army; November,1940, *WFSt;* February, 1941, Chief of Military History Department in the *OKW;* September, 1941, *Oberst;* 17th May, 1942, Representative of the *Führer* for Military History. 1st September, 1943, *Generalmajor;* 24th May, 1945, suicide in American captivity.

Adjutant: *Oberleutnant* **Wilhelm Scheidt,** born 28th August, 1912. 1938, *Leutnant der Reserve Reconnaissance* Section 6; 1941, *Oberleutnant der Reserve,* Army Military History Section; 1st April, 1944; *Rittmeister.*

# OKH

20.  *Oberbefehlshaber des Heeres* **Adolf Hitler.**

21.  *Chef des Generalstabes des Heeres* until 24th September, 1942, *General der Artillerie* **Franz Halder,** born 30th June, 1884. 1904, *Leutnant,* Bavarian 3rd Field Artillery Regiment; 1929, *Oberstleutnant;* 1st December, 1931, *Oberst;* 1st February, 1933, *Artillerie Führer VII;* 1st July, 1934, *Generalmajor;* 1st October, 1935, 7th Division; 1st August, 1936, *Generalleutnant;* 1st February, 1938, *General der Artillerie;* 27th August, 1938, *Chef des*

*Generalstabes des Heeres;* 19th July, 1940, *Generaloberst;* Retired 31st January, 1945; *Ritterkreuz.*

Franz Halder                          Kurt Zeitzer

Until 9th June/14th August, 1944, *General der Infanterie* **Kurt Zeitzler,** born 9th June, 1895. 1914, *Leutnant,* Infantry Regiment 72; 1928, *Hauptmann;* 1929, Staff, 3rd Division; 1932, Company Chief, Infantry Regiment 9; 1934, *Major* in the *Reichswehrministerium;* 1937, *Oberstleutnant;* 1939, *Oberst* and CO Infantry Regiment 60; August, 1939, Chief of the General Staff of the XXIInd Army Corps; February, 1942, *Generalmajor;* April, 1942, Chief of the General Staff, *ObWest* (Army Group D); 24th September, 1942, *General der Infanterie* (promoted over the rank of *Generalleutnant)* and Chief of the Army General Staff: 1st February, 1944, *Generaloberst;* 15th August, 1944, *Führerreserve;* 31st January, 1945, retired; *Ritterkreuz.*

Acting from 10th June, 1944 through 21st July, 1944, *Generalleutnant* **Adolf Heusinger** (see 23).

From 21st July, 1944, *Generaloberst* **Heinz Guderian,** born 17th August, 1888. 1908, *Leutnant, Jäger* Battalion 10; 1915, *Hauptmann;* December, 1918, *Grenzschutz Ost;*1922, *RWM;* 1924, General Staff, 2nd Division; 1927, *Major im RWM;* 1930, CO Motorcycle Section 3; 1931, *Oberstleutnant, RWM;* 1933, *Oberst;* 1934, Chief of Staff for the Inspectorate of Armored Troops; 1935, CO 2nd Panzer Division; 1936, *Generalmajor;* February, 1938, *Generalleutnant* and Commanding General of the *Kommando der*

*Panzertruppen;* November, 1938, *General der Panzertruppen und Chef der Schnellen Truppen;* August, 1939, Commanding General XIX Army Corps; June, 1940, Commander *Panzergruppen Guderian;* October, 1941, Commander 2nd Panzer Army; July, 1940, *Generaloberst;* December, 1941, *Führerreserve;* 20th February, 1943, *Generalinspekteur der Panzertruppen;* 21st July, 1944, Chief of the General Staff of the Army; 28th March through 1st April, 1945 on leave; *Ritterkreuz mit Eichenlaub.*

Adolf Heusinger, here in a *Bundeswehr* uniform.

Heinz Guderian

Acting from 1st April, 1945, *General der Infanterie* **Hans Krebs** (see 24)

Hans Krebs at the time of his capture by the Soviets.

22. *Adjutant des Chefs des Generalstabes des Heeres* until 9th June, 1944, *Major* **Günther Smend.**

From 25th July, 1944, *Major* **Bernd Freiherr Freytag von Loringhoven,** born 6th February, 1914. 1937, *Leutnant;* 1939, *Oberleutnant* in the 1st Panzer Division; 1940, *General Kommando* XIX Army Corps; 1942, *Hauptmann* and CO of the 2nd Section, Panzer Regiment 2; March, 1943, transferred to the command of the 111th Infantry Division; October, 1943, *Kriegsakademie;* April 1944, Operations Section, General Staff of the Army; November 1943, *Major.*

23. *Chef der Operationsabteilung im Generalstab des Heeres* until 20th July, 1944, *Generalmajor* **Adolf Heusinger,** born 4th August, 1897. 1916, *Leutnant,* Infantry Regiment 96; 1922, Adjutant, 3rd Battalion, Infantry Regiment 96; 1922, Adjutant 3rd Battalion, Infantry Regiment 15; 1927, Staff 5th Division; 1931, *RWM;* 1932, *Hauptmann;* 1934, Company Chief, Infantry Regiment 18; 1935, Operations Officer 11th Division; 1936, *Major;* April, 1937, General Staff of the Army; 1938, *Oberstleutnant;* 1940, *Oberst* and in October, Chief of the Operations Section of the Army General Staff; 1941, *Generalmajor;* 1st January, 1943, *Generalleutnant;* 10th June through 21st July, 1944 Deputy for the Chief of the Army General Staff; 22nd July through October, 1944, in Gestapo custody.

From 21st July, 1944 through 30th August 1944, *Generalleutnant* **Walter Wenck,** born 18th September, 1900. 1923, *Leutnant,* Infantry Regiment 9; 1929, Adjutant 3rd Battalion, Infantry Regiment 9; 1933, *Kriegsakademie;* 1934, *Hauptmann;* July, 1936, Staff of the *Kommando der Panzertruppen;* September, 1936, Reconnaissance Section 3; April, 1938, General Staff of XVI Army Corps; November, 1938, Chief, First Section, Panzer Regiment 2; 1939, *Major* and Operations Officer, 1st Panzer Division; 1940, *Oberstleutnant;* February, 1942, Instructor for the General Staff Training Section; June, 1942, *Oberst* and September, Chief of the General Staff of the LVII Panzer Corps; November 1942, Chief of the General Staff of the Rumanian 3rd Army; December, 1942, Chief of the General Staff of *Armee-Abteilung Hollidt;* February, 1943, *Generalmajor;* March, 1943, Chief of the General Staff of Army Group South Ukraine; 21st July, 1944, Chief of Operations Division in the General Staff of the Army; 17th February, 1945, motor vehicle accident; 7th April, 1945, *General der Panzertruppen und Führerreserve;* 16th April, 1945, CO 12th Army. *Ritterkreuz.*

**Walter Wenck**

24. *Chef der Führungsgruppe im Generalstab des Heeres* from 1st September, 1944 through 17th February/6th April, 1945, *Generalleutnant* **Walter Wenck** (see 23).

Acting from 17th February, 1945, *General der Infanterie* **Hans Krebs,** born 4th March, 1898. 1915, *Leutnant* Infantry Regiment 78; 1925, *Oberleutnant;* 1928, Chief of 13th Company, Infantry Regiment 17; 1931, *Hauptmann im RKM;* 1933, Assistant to the Military Attaché in Moscow; 1935, General Staff of the 24th Division; 1936, *Major;* 1937, General Staff of the Army; 1939, *Oberstleutnant* and in December, Chief of the General Staff of the VII Army Corps; 1940, *Oberst;* March, 1941, Deputy to the Military Attaché in Moscow; January, 1942, Chief of the General Staff of the 9th Army ; February, 1942, *Generalmajor;* March, 1943, Chief of the General Staff of Army Group Center; April, 1943, *Generalleutnant;* August, 1944, *General der Infanterie;* September, 1944, Chief of the General Staff for Army Group B; 17th February, 1945, *Chef Führungsgruppe OKH* (acting for Wenck); 1st April, 1945, Acting Head of the General Staff of the Army; surrendered to the Russians in Berlin, May 1st, 1945. *Ritterkreuz mit Eichenlaub.*

25. *Offiziere in der Operationsabteilung im Generalstab des Heeres, Oberstleutnant* **August Hermani,** born 31st May, 1911. 1934, *Leutnant;* 1938, *Oberleutnant* and Adjutant Infantry Regiment 42;

1940, *Hauptmann;* 1941, General Staff of the Army, Chief of *Transportwesen;* September, 1942, CO of the Transport Area Poltawa; November, 1942 Staff of the 304th Infantry Division; January, 1943, Major; June, 1943, Quartermaster, LII Army Corps; August, 1943, Operations Officer XXXXII Army Corps; April, 1944, *Oberstleutnant* and Operations Officer 26th Infantry Division; 10th September, 1944, General Staff of the Army, Operations Division; April, 1945, Chief of the General Staff, Reimann Corps.

*Major* **Hubertus Freiherr von Humboldt-Dachroeden,** born 24th July, 1912. 1934, *Leutnant;* 1937, *Oberleutnant;* 1938, Adjutant Arko 6; 1940, *Hauptmann* and Chief 5th Section Artillery Regiment 42; January 1942, Staff of *Harko.* 302; August, 1942, Staff of 168th Infantry Division; March, 1943, Staff Army Group B; May, 1943, *Major;* March, 1944, Operations Officer, 87th Infantry Division; 10th September, 1944 General Staff of the Army, Operations Division; April, 1945, *Führerreserve.*

*Oberstleutnant* **Ulrich de Maiziéré,** born 24th February, 1912. 1933, *Leutnant,* Infantry Regiment 5; 1935, *Oberleutnant;* 1937, Adjutant, Infantry Regiment 50; 1939, *Hauptmann;* September, 1940, Staff 18th Infantry Division; January, 1941, General Staff of the Army/ Organization Section; April, 1942, *Major;* May, 1943, Operations Officer, 10th Infantry Division; June, 1943, *Oberstleutnant;* November, 1944 as Army Operations Officer, transferred to Ob.West; 15th February, 1945, General Staff of the Army/ Operations Officer for the Operational Division; May, 1945, *WFSt.*

26. *Stellvetretender Chef des Heerespersonalamtes* (for the Chief, (see 2) until 11th October, 1944, *Generalmajor* **Wilhelm Burgdorf** (see 2).

From 12th October, 1944 to 15th January, 1945, *Generalleutnant* **Viktor Linnarz,** born 19th August, 1894. 1914, *Leutnant* Telegraph Battalion 2; 1929 left the service as *Hauptmann;* 1930, rejoined the service with Motorcycle Section 6; 1935, *Major* and CO 2nd Section, Panzer Regiment 6; 1936, Staff, *Kdo. der Panzertruppen;* 1938, *Oberstleutnant* in the *OKH/PA;* August, 1940, Oberst; June, 1941, CO of the 5th Panzer Brigade; October, 1942, Chief of Section P1, HPA; January, 1943, *Generalmajor;* April, 1944, *Generalleutnant;* 12th October, 1944, Acting Head of the *HPA;* 15th January, 1945, *Führerreserve;* March, 1945, CO 26th Panzer Division.

From 15th January, 1945, *Generalleutnant* **Ernst Maisel,** born 16th September, 1896. 1915, *Leutnant,* Bavarian 12th Field Artillery

Viktor Linnarz

Regiment; 1938, *Major* and CO 3rd Battalion, Infantry Regiment 104; 1st August, 1939, *Oberstleutnant;* 1940, Adjutant, 9th Military District; May, 1941, CO Infantry Regiment 42; October, 1941, *Oberst;* September, 1942, Section Chief in the Army Personnel Office; January, 1943, Bureau Chief in *HPA;* June, 1943, *Generalmajor;* January, 1944, *Generalleutnant;* October, 1944, Acting Chief of the Army Personnel Office; *Ritterkreuz.*

*Adjutant des Chefs HPA, Major* **Rudolf Weiss,** born 27th September, 1910. 1934, *Leutnant;* November, 1938, *OKH/ Adjutant PA;* 1940, *Hauptmann;* 1941, Adjutant, 1st Panzer Division; April 1942 attached to the Chief of Army Equipment and the Replacement Army; Adjutant General for Motorized equipment in the *AHA;* June, 1942, *Major* and from 1st October, 1942, Adjutant to the Chief of the *HPA.*

27. *Generalinspeckteur der Panzertruppen, Generaloberst* **Heinz Guderian** (see 21)

28. *Chef des Stabes des Generalinspeckteurs der Panzertruppen, Oberst* **Wolfgang Thomale,** born 25th February, 1900. 1919, *Leutnant* Motorcycle Section 3; 1926, *Oberleutnant* and Adjutant Motorcycle Section 6; 1929, Infantry School; 1933, *Hauptmann* with the Motorcycle Training Command at Zossen; 1935, Panzer Regiment 5; 1937, *Major* on the Staff of the 3rd Panzer Brigade; June, 1938, *OKH;* 1939, *Oberstleutnant;* May, 1941, CO 3rd Section Panzer Regiment 25; July, 1941, CO Panzer Regiment 27; March, 1942, *Oberst;* June, 1942 with the staff of the Chief of Army Equipment and Replacement Army; 25th February, 1943, Chief of the Staff of the General Inspector of the Panzer Troops. *Ritterkreuz.*

Wolfgang Thomale

# OKM

29. *Oberbefehlshaber der Kriegsmarine* until 30th January, 1943, *Grossadmiral Dr. h.c.* **Erich Raeder,** born 24th April, 1876. Joined the Imperial Navy, 16th April, 1894; May, 1895, Sea Cadet; April, 1900, *Oberleutnant zur See;* March, 1905, *Kapitänleutnant;* April,1911, *Korvettenkapitän;* April, 1917, *Fregattenkapitän;* November, 1919, *Kapitän zur See;* August, 1922, *Konteradmiral;* April, 1925, Vizeadmiral; October, 1928, *Admiral* and *Chef der Marine-Leitung;* 1st June, 1935, *Oberbefehlshaber der Kriegsmarine;*

Erich Raeder

20th April, 1936, *Generaladmiral;* 1st April, 1939, *Grossadmiral;* January, 1943 through April, 1945, *Admiralinspekteur der Kriegsmarine;* 1946, sentenced at Nuremberg to life in prison, released in 1955; *Ritterkreuz.*

From 30th January, 1943, *Grossadmiral* **Karl Dönitz,** born .16th September, 1991. 1913, *Leutnant zur See;* 1912, Cruiser *"Breslau;"* 1916, joined U-Boat arm; October, 1918, Prisoner of War; 1928, *Korvettenkapitän* and CO of a torpedo boat half-flotilla; 1930, Staff Officer *Marinestation Nordsee;* 1934, Commander of the Cruiser *"Emden;"* 1935, *Fregattenkapitän* and CO of the 1st U-Boat Flotilla; 1936, *Kapitän zur See* and *Führer der Unterseeboote (FdU);* 1939, *Konteradmiral und Befehlshaber der Unterseeboote (BdU);* 1940 *Vizeadmiral;* 1942, Admiral; 30th January, *Grossadmiral* and *Oberbefehlshaber der Kriegsmarine;* April, 1945, *Wehrmacht Befehlshaber Nord;* 1st May, 1945, Head of State and CIC *Wehrmacht;* 1946, sentenced to 10 years imprisonment at Nuremberg; 1956, released; *Ritterkreuz mit Eichenlaub.*

**Karl Dönitz**

30. *Begleitung des Ob.d.M. Adjutant des Ob.d.M, Kapitänleutnant* **Jan-Heinrich Hansen-Nootbaar,** born 19th April, 1911. 1935, *Leutnant zur See;* 1937, *Oberleutnant zur See;* April, 1938, First Officer on Admiralty Yacht, *"Grille;"* 1939, *Kapitänleutnant;* March, 1940, Commander of the Torpedo Boat *"Falke;"* 1941, with the 9. *Kreigeschiffbaulehrabteilung;* March, 1942, Commander *"T-22;"* May, 1943, at the disposal of the *Ob.d.M.* as Adjutant; 1st September, 1943, Adjutant to the *Ob.d.M.;* 1st October, 1943,

*Korvettenkapitän;* 27th April, 1944 acting head of the 4th Torpedo Boat Flotilla; 26th August, 1944; again Adjutant to the *Ob.d.M.;* 11th October 1944, head of the 5th Torpedo Boat Flotilla.

*Admiral beim Ob.d.M., Konteradmiral* **Gerhard Wagner,** born 23rd November, 1898. 1918, *Leutnant zur See;* 1929, *Kapitänleutnant;* 1933, *OKM;* 1935, *Korvettenkapitän* and *Wehrmachtakademie;* 1937, CO of a destroyer; 1939, *Fregattenkapitän* and Operations Officer *SKL;* 1940, *Kapitaen zur See;* June, 1941, Chief Operations Section, *SKL;* 1943, *Konteradmiral;* June, 1944, *Admiral beim Ob.d.M.*

Gerhard Wagner                    Theodor Krancke

31. *Ständiger Vertreter des Ob.d.M. im Führerhauptquartier* until 28th February, 1943, *Vizeadmiral* **Theodor Krancke,** born 30th March, 1893. 1915 *Leutnant zur See;* 1922, *Kapitänleutnant;* 1930, *Korvettenkapitän;* 1935, *Fregattenkapitän;* 1937, *Kapitän zur See* and October, CO of the Naval Academy; October, 1939, Commander of the *Panzerschiff "Admiral Scheer;"* February, 1940, *OKM/Sonderstab "Weserübung;"* April, 1940, Chief of Staff of the Commanding Admiral Norway; June, 1940, CO of the *"Admiral Scheer;"* April, 1941, *Konteradmiral;* June, 1941, Chief Quartermaster *SKL;* April, 1942, *Vizeadmiral;* 20th September, 1942, Permanent Representative of the *Ob.d.M., FHQu.;* March, 1943, *Admiral* and *Ob. Marinegruppenkommando West (kdr. Admiral Frankreich);* April, 1945, *Marineoberkommando Norwegen.*

From 1st March, 1943, *Konteradmiral* **Hans-Erich Voss,** born 30th October, 1897. 1917 *Leutnant zur See;* 1928, *Kapitänleutnant;* 1934, *Korvettenkapitän;* 1937, *Fregattenkapitän;* 1938, 3. *Marine-Unteroffizier-Lehr-Abt.;* August, 1939, *Admiralstabsoffizier, Marinegruppenkommando Ost;* November, 1939, *Kapitän zur See* and head of the *Flotten-und Ausbildungsabteilung, SKL;* January, 1942, CO, Heavy Cruiser *"Prinz Eugen;"* 1st March, 1943, *Konteradmiral und Ständiger Vertreter des Ob.d.M. im FHQu. Ritterkreuz.*

# OKL

32. *Oberbefehlshaber der Luftwaffe* until 23rd April, 1945, *Reichsmarschall* **Hermann Göring,** born 12th January, 1893. 1912, *Leutnant,* Infantry Regiment 112; 1914 Battalion Adjutant in Infantry Regiment 112; October, 1914, *Fliegertruppe* Observer with *Feldflieger Abteilung 25;* 1916, CO *Jagdstaffel 27;* June, 1918 CO *Jagdgeschwader 1, "Freiherr von Richthofen;"* 1919 as *Hauptmann* discharged; August, 1933, honorary rank of *General der Infanterie;* March, 1935, *General der Flieger und Oberbefehlshaber der Luftwaffe;* April, 1936, *Generaloberst;* February, 1938, *Generalfeldmarschall;* July, 1940, *Reichsmarschall;* 23rd April, 1945 removed from all his positions and arrested; sentenced to death at Nuremberg, committed suicide on 15th October 1946. *PlM; Ritterkreuz, Grosskreuz.*

**Hermann Göring**

From 26th April, 1945 *Generalfeldmarschall* **Robert Ritter von Greim**, born 2nd June, 1892. 16th February, 1943. *Generaloberst;* CIC *Luftflotte 6;* 25th April, 1945, *Generalfeldmarschall;* suicide on 24th May, 1945; *PLM; Ritterkreuz, Eichenlaub, Schwerter.*

Robert Ritter von Greim

33. *Chefadjutant des Ob.d.L.,* Major **Bernd von Brauchitsch**, born 30th September, 1911. 1934, *Leutnant* in Cavalry Regiment 3; 1934, transferred to the *Luftwaffe;* 1936, *Oberleutnant* in *KG 162,* *"Immelmann;"* 1939, *Hauptmann* and CO IV. *Stuka Lehr Geschwader 1;* July, 1940, Adjutant to the *Reichsmarschall;* January, 1943, Chief Adjutant of the *Ob.d.L.;* 1st March, 1943, *Oberstleutnant;* 1st March, 1944, *Oberst.*

34. *Chef des Generalstabes der Luftwaffe* until 19th August, 1943, *Generaloberst* **Hans Jeschonnek**, born 9th April, 1899. 1914, *Leutnant;* 1917, *Fliegertruppen/Jagdstaffel 40; Reichswehr, Reiter Regiments 11 und 6;* 1932, *Hauptmann;* 1933, joined the *Luftwaffe* Adjutant to Milch; *Gruppen* Commander in *KG "Hindenburg;"* 1937, *Oberstleutnant* and Chief of the Ist Section of the General Staff of the *Luftwaffe;* February, 1939, Chief of the General Staff of the *Luftwaffe;* August, 1939, *Generalmajor;* July, 1940, *General der Flieger; March,* 1942, *Generaloberst;* 19th August, 1943, suicide. *Ritterkreuz.*

From 24th August, 1943 to 22nd July, 1944, *General der Flieger* **Günther Korten**, born 26th July, 1898. 1915, *Leutnant;* 1931, *Hauptmann;* 1934, joined the *Luftwaffe;* 1934, *Major im RLM;* 1936, CO *Aufklärungsgruppe* 122; 1937 *Oberstleutnant* and Section Chief of the *RLM;* 1938, Chief of the General Staff of the

Hans Jeschonnek                    Günther Korten

Commanding General of the *Luftwaffe* in Austria; 1939, *Oberst;*
1940, Generalmajor and Chief of the General Staff of *Luftflotte 4;*
August, 1942, *Generalleutnant* and Commander of *Luftwaffe
Kommando Don;* January, 1943, *General der Flieger;* February, 1943,
Commanding General *Ist Flieger-Korps;* 24th August, 1943, Chief of
the General Staff of the *Luftwaffe;* 20th July, 1944, badly wounded
at the assassination attempt at the *FHQu* and died of his wounds on
22nd April, 1944; posthumous promotion on 23rd July, 1944 to
*Generaloberst. Ritterkreuz.*

From 1st August, 1944 to 19th September, 1944, *Generalleutnant*
**Werner Kreipe,** born 12th January, 1904. 1925 *Leutnant;* 1934,
*Hauptmann* and joined the *Luftwaffe;* 1936, *RLM;* 1937, *Major;*
1938, CO Reconnaissance Group 122;1939, *KG 2;* March, 1940,
CO III. *KG 2;* June, 1940, Section Chief in *RLM;* November, 1940,
*Oberstleutnant;* 1941, Chief of the General Staff, *Lw. Kdo. Don;*
October, 1942, Chief of Staff to the Chief *Ausbildungswesens im
RLM;* March, 1943, *Generalmajor;* July, 1943, General for
*Fliegerausbildung;* July, 1944, *Generalleutnant;* 1st August, 1944,
Chief of the General Staff of the *Luftwaffe;* 1945, CO of the
*Luftkriegsakademie.*

Acting from 29th November, 1944, *Generalleutnant* **Karl Koller,**
born 22nd February, 1898. 1917, pilot; 1920-1933, Police; 1935,
joined the *Luftwaffe;* 1936, *Major* in the General Staff of *Luftflotte 3;*
1938, *Oberstleutnant;* January, 1941, *Oberst* and Chief of the General
Staff of *Luftflotte 3;* March, 1943, *Generalmajor;* 26th August, 1943,

Werner Kreipe                    Karl Koller

Chief of the *Luftwaffenführungsstab;* May, 1944, *Generalleutnant;* 29th November, 1944, Chief of the General Staff of the *Luftwaffe* (acting); 30th January, 1945, *General der Flieger. Ritterkreuz.*

35. *Chef des Luftwaffenführungsstabes* until 31st May, 1943, *Generaloberst* **Hans Jeschonnek** ( see 39).
1st June, 1943 to 23rd August, 1942, *Generalmajor* **Karl Koller** (see 39).
From 4th September, 1944, *Generalmajor* **Eckhard Christian** (see 13).

36. *Ständiger Verbindungsoffizier des Reichsmarschalls beim Führer, General der Flieger* **Karl Bodenschatz,** born 10th December, 1890. 1912, *Leutnant;* 1916, *Oberleutnant* and joined *Fliegertruppe;* 1917, Adjutant to J.G. 1 *"Freiherr von Richthofen;"* 1919, rejoined Infantry Regiment 8; 1921 *Hauptmann;* 1932, *Major;* May, 1933, Chief of the *Luftschutzamt* in the *RWM;* September, 1933, joined the *Luftwaffe* as First Adjutant to Goering; 1934, *Oberstleutnant;* 1935/1936 also Adjutant to the *Führer* and *Reichskanzlers;* 1936, *Oberst* and Chief of the *Stabsamt/RLM;* December, 1937, Chief of the *Ministeramtes;* 1938, *Generalmajor;* September, 1939, permanent Liaison Officer of Görings with the *Führer;* January, 1941, *General der Flieger;* badly wounded at the 20th July, 1944 assassination attempt at *FHQu* and unfit for duty.

37. *Leiter der Wetterwarte beim Chef des Generalstabes der Luftwaffe, Oberregierungsrat* **Oskar Schuster,** born 31st October, 1900. 1929-

1934 student at the Technical Highschool in Munich and Dresden; 1934 *Referendar,* 1935 entered the National Weather Service; 1939 *Regierungsrat* and Chief of the Weather Service to the Chief of the General Staff of the *Luftwaffe.*

Karl Bodenschatz

# Reichsführung SS

38. *Reichsführer SS* (from 21st July, 1944, also *Chef des Heeresrüstung und Befehlshaber der Ersaztzheeres)* **Heinrich Himmler,** born 7th October, 1900. January, 1929 *Reichsführer der Schutzstaffeln;* December, 1944 through January, 1945, *Oberbefehlshaber Oberrhein,* January through March, 1945, *Oberbefehlshaber Heeres Gruppe Weichsel;* suicide in British custody on 23rd May, 1945.

39. *Verbindungsführer der Waffen-SS beim Führer* until the beginning of 1943, *SS-Obergruppenführer* **Karl Wolff,** born 13th May, 1900. 1914, *Leibgarde-Infanterie-Regiment (1. Grossherzoglich Hessisches) Nr. 115; 1931,* joined the *NSDAP* and the *SS;* 1943, *SS-Obergruppenführer und General der Waffen-SS,* Member of the Reichstag, Himmler's Personal Staff; Military Commander in Rear Area in Italy, 1944.

From October, 1943 through 1st January, 1944, *SS-Brigadeführer* **Hermann Fegelein,** born 30th October, 1906. 1932, joined the SS; 1933, *SS-Untersturmführer;* 1936, *Sturmbannführer* and CO of the SS Main Riding School; 1937, *Standartenführer;* 1940 as *Obersturmbann-führer der Reserve,* taken into the *Waffen-SS* as CO of the *SS-*

Hermann Fegelein

Below: Karl Wolff and Heinrich Himmler.

*Totenkopf-Reiter Standarte* (later *SS Kavallerie Regiment 1)*; August, 1941, CO *SS-Kavallerie-Brigade*; May, 1942, Inspector of the *SS Reit- und Fahrwesen* in the SS Main Office; December, 1942, *Oberführer* and CO *Kampfgruppe Fegelein*; April, 1943, CO *SS-Kav-Division*; May, 1943, *Brigadeführer*; 30th September, 1943, wounded and after recovery, sent to the *FHQu;* 1st January, 1944 appointed as Himmler's Liaison Officer with Hitler; 21st June, 1944, *SS-Gruppen- führer*; Vanished from Berlin on the 28th of April, 1945; US CIC reports indicate he survived the war. *Ritterkreuz, Eichenlaub, Schwerter.*

*Adjutant des Verbindungsführer der Waffen-SS, SS-Hauptsturmführer*
**Johannes Goehler,** born 15th September, 1918. 1936, joined *SS-TV*; 1941, *SS-Untersturmführer* with *SS-Reiter Regiment 1*; 1942, *SS-Obersturmführer* and Chief of the 4th Squadron, *SS-Reiter Regiment 1*; 1st September, 1943, *SS-Hauptsturmführer*; August, 1944, Adjutant to Fegelein. *Ritterkreuz.*

## Obersten Reichs- und Parteibehörden

40.  *Ständiger Beauftragter des Reichsaussenministers beim Führer, Gesandter I Klasse* **Walther Hewel,** born 25th March, 1904. 1923, Technical Highschool, Munich; 1923, Standard Bearer for the *"Stosstrupp Adolf Hitler"* during the 9th November *putsch.* Sentenced to 15 months imprisonment at Landsberg prison; Export salesman from 1927 to 1936 in Java with the Anglo Dutch Plantations of Java, Ltd.; 1933, rejoined the NSDAP via the AO; 1936, *Gauhauptstellenleiter* with the AO in Berlin; February, 1937, *Dienststelle Ribbentrop* (Head of German English Section) and *SS-Sturmbannführer*; June, 1938, joined the Foreign Office as *Legationsrat* First Class and Leader of the Personal Staff of the Foreign Minister as *SS-Standartenführer*; 1939, *Vortragender Legationsrat*; September, 1940, *Gesandter* First Class as Ministerial Director and Permanent Representative of the Foreign Minister to Hitler; 1940, *SS-Oberführer*; 1942, *SS-Brigadeführer*; 31st March, 1943, Ambassador for Special Use; vanished from Berlin before 3rd May, 1945.

National Archives

**Walther Hewel**

*Vertreter Gesandter* First Class, **Dr. Franz von Sonnleithner,** born 1st June, 1905. 1924-1928, Student of Law and Diplomacy in Vienna, Rome and Paris; 1927, Salesman; 1929, Police Directorate, Vienna; 1931, *Polizeikommissar;* 1932, Police Directorate, Salzburg; 1932, joined the NSDAP; 1934, Austrian Chancellor's Office as Code Officer; October, 1934, sentenced to 6 years at hard labor for his NSDAP activities; March, 1938, *Reichsstatthalterei Wien;* October, 1938, joined the Foreign Office as a *Legationssekretär;* 1939, *Legationsrat* in the Ministerial Office; 1941, *Vortragender Legationsrat;* 31st March, 1943, *Gesandter* First Class as Ministerial Director and acting leader of the Personal Staff of the Foreign Minister.

41. *Reichsminister für Bewaffnung und Munition* (from 2nd September, 1943 *Reichsminister für Rüstung und Kriegsproducktion),* Professor **Albert Speer,** born 19th March, 1905. Technical Highschool Karlsruhe, Munich and Berlin. Degree in Engineering; 1932, independant architecht; 1933, joined the NSDAP; 1933, *Reichspropagandaleitung;* 1934, Hitler's architect; 1937, Professor and General Building Inspector for the Capital; 1938 Prussian Privy Councillor, February, 1942, *Reichsminister* for Armaments and Munitions; Head of the OT, General Inspector for German Roadways and General Inspector for Water and Energy; May, 1942, took over the Equipment Bureau of the OKW; sentenced to 20 years imprisonment at Nuremberg.

Albert Speer

*Verbindungsmann beim Führer* from 22nd May, 1944, *Oberst* Nicolaus von Below ( see 5)

42. *Reichspresschef, Reichsleiter* **Dr. Otto Dietrich,** born 31st August, 1897. 1915, volunteer, ending as *Leutnant;* studied diplomacy and philosophy in Freiburg, Frankfurt and Munich; 1921, Doctorate in politics and trade and became business editor of the *"Essener Allg. Zeitung;"* 1928, Business Editor of the *"München-Augsburger Abendzeitung;"* 1931, joined the NSDAP and became the Editor in Chief of the *"Essener National-Zeitung;"* 1931, *Reichspresschef der NSDAP;* 1933, Vice President of the National Press Chamber; 1934, *SS-Gruppenführer;* 1936, Member of the *Reichstag;* 1938, National Press Chief and Secretary of State in the Ministry for Propaganda; 1941, *SS-Obergruppenführer;* April, 1949 in Nuermberg, sentenced to 7 years in prison, released in 1950.

Hitler, Bormann and Dr. Otto Dietrich.

*Stellvertretender Reichspresschef, Hauptdienstleiter* **Helmut Sündermann,** born 19th February, 1911. University of Munich (History, Industry and Journalism); 1930, joined the NSDAP; August, 1931, *Stabsleiter der Reichspressestelle NSDAP* and member of the SS; November, 1933, Chief of the National Socialist Party Correspondence; 1934, Leader of the Press Political Bureau of the *Reichspressechefs;* 1937, *Stabsleiter* of the *Reichspressechefs der NSDAP;* 1938, *Hauptamtsleiter* ;1941, *SS-Obersturmbannführer;* 1942, Deputy Press Chief of the Government and member of the *Reichstag.*

*DNB- Vertreter, Oberbereichsleiter* **Heinz Lorenz,** born 7th August, 1913. 1931, NSDAP; 1932 Press Stenographer, later correspondant in Wolffs Telegraphic Bureau, (from December, 1933, DNB); *HJ-Hauptbannführer;* Adjutant to the *Reichspressechef* as the News Liasion man of the DNB for foreign press material .

43.  *Adjutant des Leiters der Leiters der Partelkanzlei der NSDAP, Hauptbereichsleiter SS-Standartenfuehrer* **Wilhelm Zander,** born 22nd April 1911. Trade School, timber trade and newspaper correspondant; 1931, joined the NSDAP and SS; 1933, *Sturmführer* in the Personal Section of the *RFSS;* 1935, Adjutant *SS-Oberabschnitt Nordwest;* 1936, Adjutant, *SS-Oberabschnitt Mitte;* 1937 as *SS-Sturmbannführer* on the Staff of the Deputy of the *Führer, Reichsleiter* Bormann; 1943, *SS-Obersturmführer;* September, 1944, *SS-Standartenführer.*

# The Reichssicherheitsdienst -RSD

This organization was technically on the staff of the *Reichsführer-SS* Heinrich Himmler but he had no control over it or its members. The unit was composed of professional police personnel, trained in the protection of the *Führer* and was under the direct command of *SS-Brigadeführer* Hans Rattenhuber but all the members were under Hitler's control; all promitions and postings needing his personal approval. The members wore the uniform of the SS with blank unit collar patches on the collar, the "SD" diamond (indicating the *Sicherheitsdienst)* on the lower left sleeve. Their color of arm was police green. Founded in March of 1934 as the *Führerschutzkommando,* a name later changed to the *Reichssicherheitsdienst,* the members of this unit were responsible for the personal safety of Hitler and other top Third Reich officials including: Göring, von Ribbentrop, Himmler, Goebbels, Frick, Karl Frank, Seyss-Inquart, Terboven, Dönitz, Dr. Best, Kaltenbrunner, Ley and Koch.

They served the same role that the Mounted Rifles of the Guards did for Napoleon, accompanying Hitler on all his trips, guarding his person and his headquarters. At the military headquarters, the RSD was basically responsible for protection inside the perimeters of Hitler's personal living and work areas and the Army's *"Führer-Begleit-Kommando"* guarded the outer perimeters of the headquarters.

In Germany prior to and during the war, the Gestapo under *SS-Gruppenführer* Heinrich Müller was jointly responsible for Hitler's safety during his trips and public speeches. Gestapo members mixed with the crowds along the route of Hitler's parades, took persons suspected of possible violent acts into temporary custody during the event, searched public buildings and provided armed guards and snipers which were posted in and on the roofs of buildings along his route of travel as well as protecting the perimeters of any building he entered.

There were no special Gestapo units assigned to these details and the men engaged in this service were taken from the local Gestapo headquarters.

The following roster of RSD personnel is taken directly from Himmler's personal files and is dated in January of 1945.

*SS-Untersturmführer*
**Asmus, Karl**
Kriminal-Sekretär
SS-No. 385 089
Berlin-Charlottenburg, Kaiserin-Augusta Allee 42 IV

*SS-Untersturmführer*
**Bambey, Heinrich**
Kriminal-Sekretär
SS-No. 231 990
Berlin-Tempelhof, Hansakorso 9/I

*SS-Obersturmführer*
**Barthel, Friederich**
Kriminal-Sekretär
SS No. 290 273
München, Walchenseeplatz 25/2

*SS-Hauptsturmführer*
**Bastian, Joseph**
Inspecktor, Techn,
SS No. 289 963
Berlin-Mahlow-Blankenfelde, Maikowskistr. 116

*SS-Brigadeführer und Generalmajor d. Polizei*
**Baur, Hans**
Flugkapitän des Führers    Hans
  (Hitler's chief pilot)    Baur
SS No. 171 865
Neuviddersberg-Post Seefeld Obb.

*SS-Untersturmführer*
**Beck, Heinrich**
Kriminnal-Sekretär
SS No. 335 644
München 8, Barbarostr. 15

*SS-Untersturmführer*
**Berger, Paul**
Polizeisekretär
SS No. 422 375
Berlin-Reinickendorf-West, Kienhornstr. 10

*SS-Hauptsturmführer*
**Bergmüller, Johann**
Kriminal-Sekretär
SS No. 249 997
Berlin W 8, Kanonierstr. 40/I
München, Braystr.22

*SS-Hauptsturmführer*
**Bergmüller, Ludwig**
Kriminal-Bezirks-Sekretär
SS No. 249 996
München 27, Hörselbergstr. 2/I

*SS-Obersturmbannführer*
**Betz, Georg**
Flugkapitän
SS No. 404 538
Gmund a. Tegernsee,
Gemeinde Dürnbach, Am Ackernberg

*SS-Untersturmführer*
**Beyer, Walter**
Kriminal-Sekretär
SS No. 404 538
Dresden N 23, Böttgerstr. 52

*SS-Hauptsturmführer*
**Birzer, Fritz**
Kriminal-Sekretär
SS No. 2 047
Berlin, Kanonierstr. 40
München, Türkenstr. 89a

*SS-Obersturmführer*
**Bitter, Friedrich**
Kriminal-Kommissar
SS No. 290 161
Berlin-Pankow, Laudaerstr.7

*SS-Untersturmführer*
44 **Brandenburg, Franz**

Kriminal-Sekretär
SS No. 309 748
Berlin-Lankwitz, Seydlitzstr. 51c

*SS-Untersturmführer*
**Bühler, Stephan**
Kriminal-Sekretär
SS No. 292 541
München 8, Bärenwaldstr. 16

*SS-Untersturmführer*
**Bunde, Ernst**
Kriminal-Kommissar
SS No. 13 124
Berlin N 65, Fritz-Schulz-Str. 98

*SS-Obersturmführer*
**Danner, Anton**
Kriminal-Sekretär
SS No. 45 349
München, Dachauerstr. 48/III

*SS-Untersturmführer*
**Danner, Johann**
SS No. 282 479
München, Fassbänderplatz 3

*SS-Obersturmführer*
**Danner, Karl**
Kriminal-Sekretär
SS No. 276 663
Berlin W.u., Herrnstr. 15/I

*SS-Untersturmführer*
**Driessle, Johann**
SS No. 289 265
Wartingen b. Augsburg, Morellstr. 27

*SS-Obersturmführer*
**Ebnet, Alois**
Kriminal-Sekretär
SS No. 306 661

*SS-Hauptsturmführer*
**Eckold, Wilhelm**
Kriminal-Bezirks-Sekretär

SS No. 274 991
Berlin-Charlottenburg, Mommsenstr.

*SS-Untersturmführer*
**Eisgruber, Johann**
Kriminal-Beamter
SS No. 274 763
München, Arnulfstr. 196/I

*SS-Untersturmführer*
**Erdle, Richard**
Kriminal-Sekretär
SS No. 254 423
München 19, Gotelindenstr. 7/III

*SS-Obersturmführer*
**Eschbauer, Maximillian**
Polizeisekretär
SS No. 346 515
Berlin-Lichterfelde, Marschnerstr. 43/II

*SS-Untersturmführer*
**Escofier, Leonhard**
SS-No. 288 839

*SS-Hauptsturmführer*
**Friedrich, Hans**
Flugzeug*schloss*er
SS No. 455 220
Berlin SW 29 Kottbuser Damm 69

*SS-Untersturmführer*
**Forster, Johann**
Kriminal-Sekretär
SS No. 289 267
Berchtesgaden, Stanggass Haus C

*SS-Sturmbannführer*
**Forster, Ludwig**
Kriminal-Inspecktor
SS No. 242 881
Berlin, Kanonierstr. 40
München, Dankestr. 12

*SS-Untersturmführer*
**Forster, Michael**

Kriminal-Oberassistant
SS No. 292 546

*SS-Untersturmführer*
**Freitag, Johann**
SS No. 279 247
Stanggass/Berchtesgaden, Gemeinde Bischofswiesen Haus C

*SS-Hauptsturmführer*
**Germann, Hans**
Funker auf Begleitflugzug des Führers
   (Radioman on escort plane of Hitler's)
SS No. 254 519
München 59, Gross-Nebasstr. 11

*SS-Untersturmführer*
**Gerstl, Franz**
Kriminal-Sekretär
SS No. 337 385
Wien 19, Panzergasse 18/16

*SS-Obersturmführer*
**Gillhuber, Max**
Kriminal-Sekretär
SS No. 276 664
Berlin W 8, Kanonierstr. 40
München, Augustenstr. 65

*SS-Hauptsturmführer*
**Glaubitz, Kurt**
techn. Inspektor
SS No. 340 561
Berlin-Spandau, Oberhauserstr. 9

*SS-Obersturmführer*
**Grad, Josef**
Kriminal-Assistent
SS No. 2 318
München 23, Stenglerstr. 2/I

*SS-Untersturmführer*
**Grill, Franz**
SS No. 47 274
Berlin W 9, Hermann Göringstr. 5/III

*SS-Untersturmführer*
**Gruber, Josef**
Kriminal-Sekretär
SS No. 358 066
München 12, Kasmairstr. 71/II

*SS-Sturmbannführer*
**Guckenberger, Hans**
SS-Kriminal-Inspektor
SS No. 275 662
Berlin, Hohenzollerndamm, 190/3 lk.

*SS-Untersturmführer*
**Günzel, Hermann**
Kriminal-Sekretär
SS No. 262 808
Berlin W 35, Grossgörschenstr. 25/4

*SS-Obersturmführer*
**Hammerl, Sebastian**
Kriminal-Sekretär
SS No. 276 156
Gmund/Tegernsee, Münchner Str. 153

*SS-Untersturmführer*
**Hassenstein, Hans-Joachim**
SS-Führer, Kriminal-Kommando
SS No. 139 996
Berlin-Wilmersdorf, Sodenerstr. 12

*SS-Hauptsturmführer*
**Hausner, Josef**
SS-Kriminal-Oberassistant
SS No. 1 733
München 27, Schumannstr. 13/IV

*SS-Hauptsturmführer*
**Heinecke, Paul**
Kriminal-Kommissar
SS No. 326 396
*Schloss* Hubertusstock a. Werbelinsee

*SS-Sturmbannführer*
**Henke, Paul**
Flugkapitän
SS No. 293 539

Berlin-Schönrberg, Hewaldstr. 6

*SS-Untersturmführer*
**Henschel, Josef**
Kriminal-Sekretär
SS No. 280 570
München, Hans Mielichstr. 22/II

*SS-Obersturmführer*
**Hinz, Erwin**
Flugzeugfunker
SS No. 457 600
Hamburg-Fuhlsbüttel, Kurveneck 6/II

*SS-Sturmbannführer*
**Peter Högl**
Kriminal-Kommissar (Head of Hitler's personal guard)
SS No. 249 998
München, Schleissheimerstr. 200/III
Prinzregentenplatz 15/0

*SS-Hauptsturmführer*
**Hösl, Josef**
Kriminal-Sekretär
SS No. 254 435
Berlin-Schmargendorf, Wangerooger Steig 90
Beverstedterweg 1/3

*SS-Obersturmführer*
**Hoffmann, Max**
SS-Führer, Kriminal-Kommando
SS No. 276 319
Berlin-Hermsdorf, Mühlenfeldstr. 3

*SS-Untersturmführer*
**Hohmann, Werner**
Kriminal-Sekretär
SS No. 309 455
Berlin-Halensee, Joachim-Friedrich-Str. 29

*SS-Untersturmführer*
**Hubinger, Johann**
Kriminal-Sekretär
SS No. 289 268
Berchtesgaden, Königsseerstr. 9

*SS-Hauptsturmführer*
**Hunn, Bernhard**
Flugzeugmaschinist
SS No. 276 843
Berlin-Templehof, Albrechtstr.20

*SS-Untersturmführer*
**Ingrish, Walter**
Kriminal-Sekretär
SS No. 356 788
Wien I, Elisabethstr. 22/8

*SS-Untersturmführer*
**Jaeschke, Hugo**
Kriminal-Sekretär
SS No. 307 416
Berlin-Niederschönhauser, Bismarckplatz 4

*SS-Untersturmführer*
**Janssen, Karl**
Kriminal-Sekretär
SS No. 326 579
Berlin-Pankow, Neumannstr. 46/III

*SS-Hauptsturmführer*
**Jörg, Josef**
Kriminal-Bezirks-Sekretär
SS No. 249 994
München, Breisacherstr. 11/II

*SS-Untersturmführer*
**Just, Richard**
Kriminal-Sekretär
SS No. 367 072
Berlin-Adlershof, Kaiser-Wilhelm-Str, 60

*SS-Obersturmführer*
**Keller, Georg**
Kriminal-Assistent
SS No. 3 408
München 38, Langemarschstr. 8

*SS-Untersturmführer*
**Kennerknecht, Christian**
Kriminal-Oberassistent

SS No. 307 838
Essen, Norbertstr. 177

*SS-Sturmbannführer*
**Kiermaier, Josef**
Kriminal-Sekretär
SS No. 276 155
Gmund/Tegernsee, Tegernseestr. 101

*SS-Sturmbannführer*
**Kiesel, Paul**
Regierungs-Inspektor
SS No. 257 215

*SS-Untersturmführer*
**Knorr, Anton**
SS-Führer, Kriminal-Kommando
SS No. 335 646
Berlin W 8, Kanonierstr. 40

*SS-Untersturmführer*
**Köhler, Karl**
Kriminal-Sekretär
SS No. 292 543
Berlin W 8, Taubenstr. 53/III

**Josef Kiermaier, Heinrich Himmler's Bodyguard.**

*SS-Untersturmführer*
**Korn, Walter**
Kriminal-Sekretär
SS No. 314 352
Berlin-Adlershof, Auguste-Viktoriastr. 100

*SS-Untersturmführer*
**Kranzusch, Max**
Kriminal-Sekretär
SS No. 337 401
Berlin N.58, Senefelderstr. 10

*SS-Untersturmführer*
**Kratzer, Franz**
Kriminal-Oberassistent
SS No. 292 544
Berlin W 9, Hermann Göringstr. 5/III

*SS-Untersturmführer*
**Krick, Kurt**

SS-Führer, Kriminal-Kommando
SS No. 276 666
Berlin SW 11, Kochstr. 64

*SS-Untersturmführer*
**Kriebeler, Kurt**
SS-Führer, Kriminal-Kommando
SS No. 314 349
Berlin N 20, Heidebrinkerstr. 2

*SS-Hauptsturmführer*
**Küffner, Johann**
Kriminal-Beamter
SS No. 249 245
Obersalzberg/Berchtesgaden, Haus "Türken"
München, Potschnerstr. 16

*SS-Obersturmführer*
**Lang, Karl**
Kriminal-Sekretär
SS No. 279 245
Berchtesgaden, Marktplatz 15

*SS-Obersturmführer*
**Lauerwald, Heinrich**
techn. Inspektor
SS No. 292 416
Berlin-Mahlow-Blankenfelde, Maikowskistr. 112

*SS-Hauptsturmführer*
**Leciejewski, Paul**
Flugzugfunker
SS No. 177 000
München 59, Wasserturmstr. 9

*SS-Untersturmführer*
**Lorenz, Nikolaus**
SS-Führer, Kriminal-Kommando
SS No. 331 957

*SS-Hauptsturmführer*
**Lutz, Franz**
Kriminal-Oberinspektor
SS No. 249 999

Grünwald b. München, Major-Humser-Str. 3

*SS-Untersturmführer*
**Madsack, Erich**
SS-Führer, Kriminal-Kommando
SS No. 36 030
Berlin-Neuköllin, Boddinstr. 27/IV

*SS-Obersturmführer*
**Manthey, Karl**
Kriminal-Sekretär
SS No. 278 667
Berlin SW 68, Kochstr. 64/I

*SS-Untersturmführer*
**Maurer, Alfred**
Kriminal-Sekretär
SS No. 356 787

*SS-Untersturmführer*
**Meier, Helmut**
Kriminal-Sekretär
SS No. 275 535
Berlin-Lichterfelde, Raabestr. 6

*SS-Untersturmführer*
**Meissner, Paul**
SS-Führer, Kriminal-Kommando
SS No. 282 100

*SS-Untersturmführer*
**Meister, Karl**
Kriminal-Kommissar
SS No. 279 244
München, Diedesheimerstr. 24/I

*SS-Untersturmführer*
**Müller, Johann**
Kriminal-Sekretär
SS No. 278 588
München, Zaubstr. 3/I

*SS-Untersturmführer*
**Müller, Karl**
Kriminal-Sekretär
SS No. 279 250
Berlin-Tempelhof, Götzstr. 12/0

*SS-Untersturmführer*
**Mundt, Alfred**
Kriminal-Oberassistent
SS No. 150 678
Berlin SW 61, Grossbeerenstr. 19/III

*SS-Untersturmführer*
**Neidel, Franz**
SS-Führer, Kriminal-Kommando
SS No. 331 958
München, Budliebstr. 10/I

*SS-Hauptsturmführer*
**Nein, Hermann**
Flugkapitän, Begleitmaschine des Führers
SS No. 337 816
Berlin-Halensee, Kurfürstendamm 150/I
Erlangen, Am Eichenwald 6

*SS-Hauptsturmführer*
**Noack, Ernst**
Polizei-Inspektor
SS No. 289 232
Berlin-Neukölln, Selkestr. 24a

*SS-Obersturmführer*
**Oppelt, Alois**
Kriminal-Hauptwachtmeister
SS No. 263 542
München, Innere-Wienerstr. 16/I

*SS-Untersturmführer*
**Ortner, Johann**
SS-Führer, Kriminal-Kommando
SS No. 279 253
Berchtesgaden-Stangass, Gemeinde Bischofswiesen

*SS-Untersturmführer*
**Osswald, Emil**
Flugzeugfunker
SS No. 457 253
Berlin W 50. Ranke Str. 19/III

*SS-Untersturmführer*
**Osterhuber, Sebastian**
Kriminal-Sekretär

SS No. 231 995
Berlin-Tiergarten, Schleswiger-Ufer 9/II

*SS-Untersturmführer*
**Portner, Joseph**
SS-Führer, Kriminal-Kommando
SS No. 254 484
München 5, Baaderstr. 1/II

*SS-Brigadeführer*
**Rattenhuber, Hans**
Oberst d. Polizei, Kriminal-Kommando
SS No. 52 877
München, Lindenstr. 29
Schaftlach b/ München, Haus Nr. 110

*SS-Untersturmführer*
**Rausch, Franz**
SS-Führer, Kriminal-Kommando
SS No. 291 303
Berlin W 8, Kanonierstr 40.

*SS-Untersturmführer*
**Resch, Xaver**
SS-Führer, Kriminal-Kommando
SS No. 279 255
München, 9, Cammabichstr. 11/II

*SS-Hauptsturmführer*
**Röpert, Werner**
Techn. Inspektor
SS No. 46 867
Haar b. München, Defreggerstr. 2

*SS-Untersturmführer*
**Roganz, Wili**
Kriminal-Sekretär
SS No. 308 043
Berlin-Neukölln, Boddinstr.15

*SS-Untersturmführer*
**Schlammer, Anton**
Kriminal-Oberassistent
SS No. 280 489
München-Pasing, Zündterstr. 16

National Archives

**Hans Rattenhuber, promoted to** *SS-Gruppenführer* **on February 24, 1945.**

*SS-Untersturmführer*
**Schlemmer, Hermann**
Kriminal-Sekretär
SS No. 272 405
München 5, Dreimühlenstr. 17/III

*SS-Untersturmführer*
**Schmid, Eduard**
Kriminal-Sekretär
SS No. 289 264
München 22, Bürkleinstr. 10/I

*SS-Sturmbannführer*
**Schmidtbauer, Konrad**
Kriminal-Beamter
SS No. 250 001
München 59, Häherweg 34/I
Stangafl, Gemeinde Bishofswiesen,
Ld.-Krs. Berchtesgaden

*SS-Sturmbannführer*
**Schmidt, Friedrich**
Kriminal-Inspektor
SS No. 250 000
München 8, Spireestr. 5

*SS-Obersturmführer*
**Schmidt, Georg**
Kriminal-Inspektor
SS No. 279 246
Bad-Reichenhall, Tirolerstr. 1/I

*SS-Untersturmführer*
**Schmidt, Johann**
Kriminal-Sekretär
SS No. 275 534
Berlin-Spandau, Ulmenstr. 9/III

*SS-Untersturmführer*
**Schneller, Hugo**
Kriminal-Sekretär
SS No. 231 981
Berlin-Tempelhof, Löwenhardtdamm 39

*SS-Untersturmführer*
**Scholz, Konrad**

Kriminal-Sekretär
SS No. 280 091
Berlin-Charlottenburg, Havelstr. */I

*SS-Untersturmführer*
**Schülein, Karl**
Kriminal-Sekretär
SS No. 231 980
Grünwald b. München, Eierwiese 26

*SS-Untersturmführer*
**Schumm, Paul**
Kriminal-Obersekretär
SS No. 280 490
Berlin W 9, Hermann Göringstr. 5/III

*SS-Untersturmführer*
**Schwägler, Martin**
Kraftfahrer
SS No. 4 846
München, Briennerstr. 50

*SS-Obersturmführer*
**Sebald, Albert**
Kriminal-Sekretär
SS No. 279 252
Berlin-Schmargendorf, Beverstedterweg 8/II

*SS-Untersturmführer*
**Seibert, Joseph**
Kriminal-Sekretär
SS No. 276 154
Berlin W 9, Hermann Göringstr. 5/III

*SS-Untersturmführer*
**Stummer, Johann**
SS-Führer, Kriminal-Kommando
SS No. 279 256
Berlin NO 18, Landsberger Alleee 126/II

*SS-Untersturmführer*
**Volk, Joseph**
Kriminal-Sekretär
SS No. 353 336
Berlin W 8, WIlhelmstr. 73

*SS-Untersturmführer*
**Vollnhals, Georg**
Kriminal-Sekretär
SS No. 279 256
Berlin NO 18, Landsberger Allee 126/II

*SS-Sturmbannführer*
**Weber, Johann**
Verwaltungsbeamter, Kriminal-Kommando
SS No. 276 029
Berlin-Tempelhof, Kaiserin-Augusta-Allee 18

*SS-Obersturmführer*
**Weckerling, Karl**
Kriminal-Angestellter
SS No. 483
Berlin W 8, Kanonierstr. 40
München-Schwabing, Rheinstr. 20/IVm

*SS-Untersturmführer*
**Windisch, Hans**
Kriminal-Sekretär
SS No. 357 073
Berlin W 8, Taubenstr. 53/III

*SS-Hauptsturmführer*
**Windorfer, Johann**
Kriminal-Bezirks-Sekretär
SS No. 248 061
München, Richard-Strauflstr. 3/III

*SS-Hauptsturmführer*
**Wolf, Hans**
Tech.Oberinspektor
SS No. 279 443
Kol. Badheim, Post Vatersetten, Krs. Ebersberg, Gartenstr. 214

*SS-Sturmbannführer*
**Zaske, Ernst**
Kriminal-Assistent
SS No. 1 338
München, Äussere Prinz Regentenstr, 71/IV

*SS-Untersturmführer*
**Zenger, Karl**
Kriminal-Oberassistent

SS No. 277 240
Salzburg, Haus Ottenstein

*SS-Obersturmführer*
**Zimmer, Karl**
Kriminal-Sekrertär
SS No. 275 532
Berlin-Neukölln, FLughafenstr. 31/III

*SS-Hauptsturmführer*
**Zimmermann, Erich**
SS -Führer, Kriminal-Kommando
SS No. 340 662
München 25, Immerkoflerstr. 40

*SS-Hauptsturmführer*
**Zintel, Max**
SS No. 177 001
Flieger/Regierungs-Oberinsspektor
SS No. 177 001
München, Lampadiusstr. 30/III

*SS-Untersturmführer*
**Zollner, August**
Kriminal-Sekretär
SS No. 288 840
München, Asgardstr 25/3

# Hitler's Military Headquarters and Movements, 1939-1945

## 1939

*3rd through 19th September, 1939,* Poland, *Sonderzug* (Special Train).
*19th through 25th September, 1939, Zoppot* (Hotel Casino).

**Hitler travels by train to view the Polish campaign.**

*26th September, 1939,* Hitler returned to Berlin.
*28th September, 1939,* Hitler visited Wilhelmshaven to greet returning U-
    Boat crews.
*5th October, 1939,* Hitler flew from Berlin to Warsaw, landing at Warsaw's
    O Kecei airport at 11:30 AM. He reviewed a victory parade and
    returned to Berlin on the same day.

Hitler greets the victorious U-Boat crews at Wilhelmshaven, one of which sank the British aircraft carrier *"Courageous"* (U-47, commanded by Günther Prien).

The victory parade in Warsaw.

*8th November, 1939,* Hitler went by *Sonderzug* to Munich to celebrate the annual 9 November, 1923 *Putsch.* A bomb explosion at the *Bürgerbräukeller* immediately following Hitler's speech killed and injured a number of participants.

*9th November, 1939,* Hitler returned to Berlin.

Hitler speaks at the Munich *Bürgerbräukeller* on November 9.

*11th November, 1939,* Hitler returned to Munich for memorial services
for those killed on the 8th: Michael Wilhelm Kaiser, Emil
Kasberger, Franz Lutz, Leonhard Reindl, Eugen Schachta,
Michael Schmeidl and Wilhelm Weber.

*12th November, 1939,* Hitler returned to Berlin.

Memorial services in front of the *Feldherrnhalle* on November 11.

*26th November, 1939,* Hitler returned to Munich to visit the wounded in hospital.

*28th November, 1939,* Hitler was back in Berlin.

*6th December, 1939,* Hitler visited *Generalfeldmarschall a.D.* von Mackensen at his estate at Brüssow in honor of the WWI commander's 90th birthday and returned to Berlin the same day.

*23rd through 25th December, 1939,* Hitler visited troops on the West Front at Hunsruck and Saarbrucken. He also paid a special visit to Infantry Regiment 199 that carried the traditions for the former Bavarian Infantry Regiment "List" in whose ranks Hitler had served in World War 1.

Memorial leaflet for the Inf. Rgt. "List" Christmas celebration.

Hitler with members of the *Luftwaffe*.

# 1940

*24th February, 1940,* Hitler went to Munich to give a speech at the *Hofbräuhaus* marking the anniversary of the proclamation of the NSDAP program in 1920.

*17th March, 1940,* Hitler went by *Sonderzug* to the Brenner Pass to meet with Mussolini.

Mussolini and Hitler at the Brenner Pass.

*19th March, 1940,* Hitler was in Berlin.

*9th May, 1940,* Hitler left Berlin in his *Sonderzug.*

*10th May through 6th June, 1940,* Hitler was at his headquarters *"Felsennest"* near Münstereifel for the Campaign in the West.

Hitler and his staff at the "Felsennest" FHQ.

*6th June through 28th June, 1940,* Hitler moved his headquarters to *"Wolfsschlucht"* at Bruly-le-Peche in Belgium.

*28th June through 5th July, 1940,* Hitler's headquarters was at "Tannenberg" in the Schwarzwald.

*6th July, 1940,* Hitler returned to Berlin by *Sonderzug* to a triumphal welcome.

Hitler is driven through Berlin after the fall of France.

*23rd July, 1940,* Hitler went to Beyreuth to attend the Wagner Festival.

*26th July, 1940,* Hitler went to the Obersalzburg.

*6th August, 1940,* Hitler returned to Berlin.

*7th August, 1940,* Hitler went to Essen and presented the first Pionier of Labor award and the Gold Party Badge to Gustav Krupp on his 70th birthday, and from there went to the Obersalzburg.

*2nd September, 1940,* Hitler returned to Berlin.

Hitler opens the 2nd Winter War Winter Help program on September 4.

*3rd October, 1940,* Hitler travelled in his *Sonderzug* to the Brenner Pass for a meeting with Mussolini. From there, Hitler went to the Obersalzburg.

Hitler meets with Mussolini at the Brenner Pass on October 4.

*14th October, 1940,* Hitler was back in Berlin.

*21st October, 1940,* Hitler left Berlin in his *Sonderzug* for France.

*22nd October, 1940,* Hitler had a conference at Montoire, a small French town located between Tours and Vendome for a conference with Pierre Laval.

*23rd October, 1940,* Hitler arrived by *Sonderzug* at Hendaye on the Franco-Spanish border for a conference with Francisco Franco and Marshal Petain.

Hitler and Petain.

Hitler and Franco.

*24th October, 1940,* Hitler returned to Germany but stopped at the Belgian border after receiving news of Mussolini's invasion of Greece. The *Sonderzug* then proceeded south towards Italy so that Hitler could confer with Mussolini.

*28th October, 1940,* Hitler arrived in Florence for a two hour conference with Mussolini.

*31st October, 1940,* Hitler arrived back in Berlin.

*8th November, 1940,* Hitler went to Munich for the 9th November ceremonies.

Hitler in Munich on November 9.

*9th November, 1940,* Hitler returned to Berlin.

*16th November, 1940,* Hitler left for the Obersalzburg.

*20th November, 1940,* Hitler went to Vienna for the signing of documents which added Hungary to the Three Power Pact.

*22nd November, 1940,* Hitler received a Rumanian delegation in Berlin for a conference regarding the inclusion of Rumania in the Three Power Pact.

*27th November, 1940,* Hitler went to Munich for a meeting with Mussolini.

*3rd December, 1940,* Hitler was back in Berlin.

*23rd December, 1940,* Hitler went by *Sonderzug* to make his Christmas visits to his troops. He visited units at Calais, Boulogne and Paris.

*27th December, 1940,* Hitler returned to Berlin.

Hitler and General Antonescu of Romania in Berlin on November 23.

# 1941

*1st January, 1941,* Hitler went to the Obersalzburg.
*17th January, 1941,* Hitler had a conference in Salzburg with Mussolini.
*29th January, 1941,* Hitler was back in Berlin.
*14th February, 1941,* Hitler returned to the Obersalzburg.

Hitler speaks in Munich on February 25 while staying at the Obersalzburg.

*1st March, 1941,* Hitler went to Vienna for ceremonies marking the inclusion of Bulgaria in the Three Power Pact.

*4th March, 1941,* Hitler was back at the Obersalzburg.

*12th March, 1941,* Hitler was in Linz for ceremonies held to mark the anniversary of the 1938 *Anschluss* between Germany and Austria.

**Hitler's motorcade in Linz, Austria.**

*16th March, 1941,* Hitler was once again in Berlin.

*21st March, 1941,* Hitler went by *Sonderzug* to Munich where he conferred with the Hungarian Foreign Minister von Bardossy.

*25th March, 1941,* Hitler went to Vienna for ceremonies including Jugoslavia in the Three Power Pact.

*26th March, 1941,* Hitler returned to Berlin.

*12th April through 26th April, 1941,* Hitler was in his *Sonderzug* at his military headquarters *"Frühlingssturm"* at a railroad sideline near Mönchskirchen in the Steiermark for the Balkans Campaign.

**While at *"Frühlingssturm"* FHQu Hitler met with Admiral von Horthy of Hungary.**

*26th April, 1941,* Hitler went by train to Graz and also visited Marburg.
*27th April, 1941,* Hitler visited Klangenfurt.
*28th April, 1941,* Hitler returned to Berlin.

On May 4 Hitler reports to the Reichstag on the Balkan campaign.

*5th May, 1941,* Hitler went to the Obersalzburg.
*13th May, 1941,* Hitler flew to Berlin to address an emergency meeting of *Reichsleiters* and *Gauleiters* about the flight of Deputy *Führer* Rudolf Hess to England.
*13th of May, 1941,* Hitler returned to the Obersalzburg.
*2nd June, 1941,* Hitler met with Mussolini at the Brenner Pass.
*6th of June, 1941,* Hitler was back at the Obersalzburg.

King Boris of Bulgaria meets with Hitler at the Obersalzburg in early June.

Hitler meets General Antonescu in Munich.

*12th of June, 1941,* Hitler was in Munich for a conference with Romanian leader General Antonescu.

*24th June, 1941 through 7th November, 1941,* Hitler was based at his military headquarters *"Wolfsschanze"* at Rastenberg in East Prussia for the campaign against the Soviet Union.

Hitler and Werner Mölders at Rastenberg in mid-July, 1941. Mölders has just received his Oakleaves, Swords and Diamonds to his Knight's Cross.

*28th August, 1941,* Hitler went to Uman in the Ukraine to meet with Mussolini and inspect Italian troops fighting in Russia.

Hitler and Mussolini in the Ukraine.

*29th August, 1941,* Hitler returned to the *"Wolfsschanze."*

*24th September, 1941,* Hitler went to Borrisow in Russia to visit Army Group Center and confer with Field Marshal von Bock.

*2nd October, 1941,* Hitler went to Berlin to deliver a speech about the progress of the campaign in Russia.

Hitler speaking in Berlin on October 3.

*4th October, 1941,* Hitler returned to the *"Wolfsschanze."*

*7th November, 1941,* Hitler went to Munich for ceremonies marking the *Putsch.*

Hitler speaking at the *Löwenbräukeller* in Munich on November 9.

*11th November, 1941,* Hitler was again at the "*Wolfsschanze.*"

*21st November, 1941,* Hitler was in Berlin to attend the funeral services for Luftwaffe General Udet.

*28th November, 1941,* Hitler attended the funeral of *Luftwaffe* fighter ace Werner Mölders at the Air Ministry in Berlin.

*29th November, 1941,* Hitler returned to the "*Wolfsschanze.*"

*2nd December, 1941,* Hitler flew to Poltava, Russia, for a conference at Army Group South.

*4th December, 1941,* Hitler returned to the "*Wolfsschanze.*"

*9th December, 1941,* Hitler went to Berlin for a meeting with the Grand Mufti of Jerusalem.

The Grand Mufti of Jerusalem and Hitler on December 9.

Four days after Pearl Harbor, Germany declares war in the United States.

*11th December, 1941,* Hitler delivered a speech at the *Reichstag* declaring war on the United States.

*16th December, 1941,* Hitler was back in the "*Wolfsschanze.*"

# 1942

*12th February, 1942,* Hitler was in Berlin for the funeral of Dr. Fritz Todt who had died at the "*Wolfsschanze*" in a mysterious courier plane crash on February 8.

Hitler places a wreath in front of Dr. Fritz Todt's coffin.

B. Kudlička

On March 15, 1942, Hitler is greeted at the entrance of the Zeughaus in Berlin by *Gross-admiral* Raeder, *Generalfeld-marschall* Keitel and *Generalfeld-marschall* Milch. This was on the occasion of the *Heldengedenktag* (Heroes' Commemoration Day) ceremonies.

*15th February, 1942,* Hitler retuned to the *"Wolfsschanze."*

*15th March, 1942,* Hitler was in Berlin to address the *"Heldengedenktag"* ceremonies.

*16th March, 1942,* Hitler was once again back in the *"Wolfsschanze."*

Hitler celebrates his 53rd birthday at his eastern *FHQu.* He is shown in conference with Göring and Keitel.

*16th April, 1942,* Hitler left Berlin in his *Sonderzug* for the Obersalzburg.

*24th April, 1942,* Hitler left for Berlin to address a meeting of the *Reichstag.*

*29th-30th April, 1942,* Hitler met with Mussolini at *Schloss* Klessheim near Salzburg.

Mussolini and Hitler at *Schloss* Klessheim.

*3rd May, 1942,* Hitler returned to the *"Wolfsschanze."*

*21st May, 1942,* Hitler went by *Sonderzug* to Berlin to attend the funeral of *Gauleiter* Röver.

*24th May, 1942,* Hitler was back at the *"Wolfsschanze."*

*28th May, 1942,* Hitler left for Berlin by *Sonderzug* and delivered a speech to officer candidates at the *Sportspalast* on the 29th.

*31st May, 1942,* Hitler returned to the *"Wolfsschanze."*

*4th June, 1942,* Hitler left by aircraft from *"Wolfsschanze"* for Finnland and a conference with Finnish leaders. Return the same day.

**Hitler meets with Marshal Mannerheim of Finland on June 4.**

*9th June, 1942,* Hitler was in Berlin for the funeral of *SS-Obergruppen-führer* Heydrich who had been murdered in Prague by British agents.

**The Heydrich funeral in Berlin.**

*10th June, 1942,* Hitler went to Munich. He attended the funeral of
NSKK leader Adolf Hühnlein on June 21.

Hitler lays a wreath at the foot of Adolf Hühnlein's coffin.

*22nd June, 1942,* Hitler returned to Berlin.
*26th June, 1942,* Hitler was once more at the *"Wolfsschanze."*
*17th July through 31st October, 1942,* Hitler had his headquarters at
*"Wehrwolf,"* Vinnitza in the Ukraine.

Croat leader Dr. Ante Pavelić visits Hitler in early September.

*28th September, 1942,* Hitler went to Berlin to give a speech to officer
candidates at the *Sportspalast.*
*4th October, 1942,* Hitler was back at *"Wehrwolf."*
*31st October, 1942,* Hitler returned to *"Wolfsschanze."* His headquarters
remained there until February 17, 1943.

On the evening of November 8 Hitler speaks to the Old Guard in Munich.

*7th November, 1942,* Hitler went by *Sonderzug* to Munich for 9th
    November ceremonies.

*23rd November, 1942,* Hitler returned to "*Wolfsschanze.*"

Spanish "Blue Division" commander Augustin Munoz-Grande receives his Oakleaves to the
Knight's Cross on December 16, 1942.

# 1943

*17th February, 1943,* Hitler flew to Saprosche for a conference with Field
    Marshal von Manstein.

Von Manstein
and Hitler.

*21st February through 13th March, 1943,* Hitler's Headquarters was at
   *"Wehrwolf."*
*10th March, 1943,* Hitler flew to Saprosche for a conference with Field
   Marshal von Manstein.
*10th March, 1943,* Hitler returned to *"Wehrwolf."*
*13th March, 1943,* Hitler moved his Headquarters back to *"Wolfsschanze."*
*20th March, 1943,* Hitler went to Berlin for *Heldengedenktag* ceremonies.
*21st March, 1943,* Hitler went to the Obersalzburg.

While at Obersalzburg Hitler celebrates his 44th birthday.

*1st May, 1943,* Hitler went to the military proving ground at Krummersdorf and inspected a number of wooden mockups of projected weapons including the giant *Maus* tank.

**Hitler at Krummersdorf.**

*7th May, 1943,* Hitler went to Berlin for funeral services for Viktor Lutze, Chief of Staff of the SA.

*21st May, 1943,* Hitler returned to the Obersalzburg.

*30th June, 1943,* Hitler was once again at *"Wolfsschanze."*

*19th July, 1943,* Hitler went to Feltre in Italy for a conference with Mussolini. 19th July, 1943, Hitler flew back to *"Wolfsschanze."*

*27th August, 1943,* Hitler flew to *"Wehrwolf"* for a conference with Manstein.

*28th August, 1943,* Hitler returned to *"Wolfsschanze."*

*8th September, 1943,* Hitler flew to Saporoshe for a conference with Army Group South.

*8th September, 1943,* Hitler returned to *"Wolfsschanze."*

*7th November, 1943,* Hitler went the *Sonderzug* to Munich for the annual ceremonies.

*17th November, 1943,* Hitler returned to *"Wolfsschanze."*

*20th November, 1943,* Hitler went to Breslau to address the annual class of Officer Candidates.

*21st November, 1943,* Hitler went to Berlin.

*7th December, 1943,* Hitler went to the Obersalzburg.

*22nd December, 1943,* Hitler was at the *"Wolfsschanze."*

# 1944

*15th March, 1944,* Hitler flew to the Obersalzburg where he met with Hungarian Chief of State Horthy at *Schloss* Klessheim on March 18.

Hitler and Horthy.

*17th April, 1944,* Hitler attended the funeral of *Gauleiter* Adolf Wagner in Munich.

*22nd April, 1944,* Hitler met with Mussolini at *Schloss* Klessheim.

*26th April, 1944,* Hitler flew to Berlin to attend the funeral of *General-oberst* Hube who had been killed in a plane crash on April 21.

Hitler attends *Generaloberst* Hube's funeral.

*12th May, 1944,* Hitler met with Slovakian leaders at *Schloss* Klessheim.

*17th June, 1944,* Hitler flew to Metz and went from there to Margival where he held a conference with Field Marshals Rommel and von Rundstedt.

*18th June, 1944,* Hitler returned to the *Berghof.*

*1st July, 1944,* Hitler returned to Berlin where he gave the eulogy for *Generaloberst* Dietl who had died in a plane crash on June 30.

Hitler eulogizes *Generaloberst* Dietl.

Hitler receives a report from the front during his last days at the *Berghof.*

*14th July, 1944,* Hitler left the Obersalzburg for the last time.

*15th July, 1944,* Hitler was once more at the *"Wolfsschanze."*

(On 20th July, 1944, an assassination attempt was made at *FHQu* but was unsuccessful.)

Bormann, Göring, Hitler and Himmler after the assassination attempt. Note the bandage on Hitler's left hand.

*20th November, 1944,* Hitler left the *"Wolfsschanze"* for the last time, moving his headquarters to Berlin.

*11th December, 1944,* Hitler went to *"Adlershorst"* for the Ardennes Offensive.

# 1945

*15th January, 1945,* Hitler returned to Berlin.

*11th March, 1945,* Hitler made a day's trip to the Oder front, east of Berlin.

Hitler during one of his last visits to the front. To his right is his pilot, Hans Baur.

Hitler on the Oder front on March 11.

# Hitler's official visits to areas outside of Germany, September 1, 1939-June 17, 1944.

**1939**

| | |
|---|---|
| 4th September | Kulm and the Polish Corridor area |
| 5th September | Polish Corridor area |
| 6th September | Tuchler Heath |
| 7th through 10th September | Polish Corridor area |
| 11th September | Area of Lodz & Rava |
| 13th September | Lodz |
| 14th September | Polish Corrodor |
| 15th September | Galacia (Jaroslav and Ubieszyn) |
| 16th through 18th September | Galacia and Polish Corridor area |
| 19th September | Oliva, Zoppot and Danzig |
| 20th September | Zoppot |
| 21st September | Westerplate, Gdingen and Oxhöft |
| 22nd September | Praga/Warsaw, Zoppot |
| 23rd through 24th September | Zoppot |
| 25th September | Zoppot, Bzura area |
| 5th October | Warsaw |
| 24th December | Spichern area |

**1940**

| | |
|---|---|
| 18th March | Brenner-Innsbruck |
| 24th May | Charleville |
| 2nd June | Langemarck, Vimy Heights, Loretto |
| 3rd through 25th June | Bruly le Peche |
| 21st June | Compiegne |
| 23rd June | Paris |
| 26th through 27th June | Northern France |
| 29th June | Strassburg-Schlettstadt |
| 30th June | Mülhausen & Upper Alsace |
| 4th October | Brenner |
| 22nd October | Montoire sur le Loir |
| 23rd October | Hendaye |
| 24th October | Montoire sur le Loir |
| 25th October | Yvoir in Belgium |
| 28th October | Florence in Italy |
| 20th November | Vienna |
| 23rd December | Area of Calais-Boulonge |
| 24th December | Area of Abbéville |
| 25th December | Area north of Paris |
| 26th December | Northern France |

**1941**

| | |
|---|---|
| 19th January | Salzburg |

| | |
|---|---|
| 1st March | Vienna |
| 11th through 25th April | Mönchskirchen |
| 26th April | Graz-Marburg a.d. Drau |
| 27th April | Klagenfurt |
| 2nd June | Brenner |
| 26th August | Brest-Litowsk |
| 27th August | Gorsk |
| 28th August | Uman |
| 24th September | Borissow |
| 2nd December | Kiev, Maripol, Mius |
| 3rd December | Mariopol-Poltava |
| 4th December | Poltava |

## 1942
| | |
|---|---|
| 29th through 30th April | Klessheim-Salzburg |
| 4th June | Micheli in Finland |
| 17th through 31st October | Vinniza in Ukraine |

## 1943
| | |
|---|---|
| 17th through 19th February | Saporoshe |
| 19th through 13th March | Vinniza |
| 10th March | Saporoshe |
| 13th March | Smolensk |
| 7th through 10th April | Klessheim |
| 12th April | Klessheim |
| 16th through 17th April | Klessheim |
| 23rd April | Klessheim |
| 27th April | Klessheim |
| 29th April | Klessheim |
| 19th July | Feltre in Italy |
| 27th August | Vinniza |
| 8th September | Saporoshe |

## 1944
| | |
|---|---|
| 18th March | Klessheim |
| 22nd through 23rd April | Klessheim |
| 12th May | Klessheim |
| 17th June | Metz-Margival |

# Hitler's First Wartime Headquarters: The *Führersonderzug* (1939-1945)

After German troops crossed the German-Polish border on September 1, 1939, the *Führer-Begleit-Bataillon* (FBB) moved into position to establish and secure a headquarters for Hitler in the vicinity of the border. The preparations for this move were begun on August 23, 1939 under the code name *"Führerreise"* (Leader's trip). Under the leadership of the Commanding Officer of the *FHQu*, *Generalmajor* Erwin Rommel, three groups were constituted; one for the security and control of the railroad right of way over which Hitler's *Sonderzug* (Special Train) was expected to travel, the second as a reserve and the third as a *Frontgruppe* (Frontline Group) to protect Hitler's visits to the operational areas. The first area for the command train was the railroad station in Bad Polzin and on the first day of the war, a 500 meter perimeter was established. The commanding officer of the headquarters was notified by Hitler's army adjutant, *Hauptmann* Engel, that Hitler's train would arrive in Bad Polzin on September 4.

On the evening of September 3, the command train left Berlin for the Polish front. In Hitler's entourage was found, in addition to his military adjutants, liaison officers and various Party officials, the Chief of the *Oberkommando der Wehrmacht, Generaloberst* Keitel and the Chief of the *Wehrmachtführungsamtes (WFA), Generalmajor* Jodl. The command train arrived at Bad Polzin at 1:56 am.

The *Führerzug* had been prepared in 1938 in case of mobilization and at the outbreak of the war was called the *"Führerhauptquartier"* and later

During the war the sequence of cars changed slightly. The *Führer's* Pullman, the dining car and the sleeping cars could be connected with the postal telephone network during stops.

**17 Flakwagon**

90

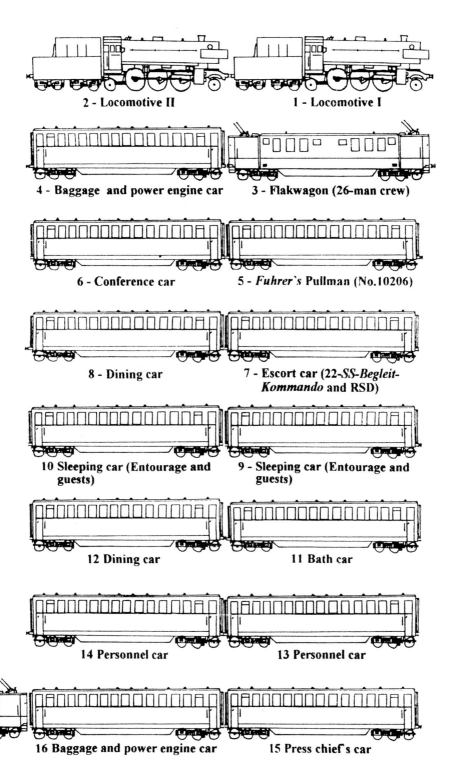

2 - Locomotive II                 1 - Locomotive I

4 - Baggage and power engine car       3 - Flakwagon (26-man crew)

6 - Conference car            5 - *Fuhrer*'s Pullman (No.10206)

8 - Dining car              7 - Escort car (22-*SS-Begleit-Kommando* and RSD)

10 Sleeping car (Entourage and       9 - Sleeping car (Entourage and
guests)                     guests)

12 Dining car                 11 Bath car

14 Personnel car               13 Personnel car

16 Baggage and power engine car     15 Press chief's car

(Illustration courtesy I.M. Baxter Collection.)

was given the code name *"Amerika."* It consisted of two steam locomotives, an anti-aircraft car with one 20 cm anti aircraft gun, baggage car, command car, signals car, a combination sleeping car and office area for Hitler, an escort commando car, dining car, a number of guest and sleeping cars a press car and another anti aircraft car.

On September 4 at 9:30AM, Hitler made his first front line visit which went from Neustettin to Komierow where Hitler was oriented at the at the headquarters of the 4th Army.

After a noon meal from the field kitchen, the entourage continued its journey through the Tuchler heath.

On September 5, the *Führer* train arrived at *Gross-Born*. From here, Hitler made a number of visits to the front, for example the advance route of the 3rd Panzer Division which was littered with the remains of a Polish division.

On September 8, the train arrived at Illnau bei Oppeln and from there, Hitler made further front visits to various command posts.

Hitler in conversation with the Commanding Officer of the 30th Infantry Division, *Generalleutnant* von Briesen after the battle on the Bzura.

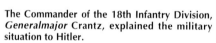

The Commander of the 18th Infantry Division, *Generalmajor* Crantz, explained the military situation to Hitler.

From left to right: *General der Artillerie* von Reichenau, *Generalmajor* Rommel, *Reichsleiter* Bormann, Hitler, Crantz, Hitler's adjutant, *Hauptmann* Engel.

On September 10th, Hitler visited the headquarters of the 10th Army at Bialaczow. Hitler was briefed by von Reichenau. From left to right: Keitel, Hitler, Rommel, von Reichenau (with the scissors telescope).

Another visit to an operational area was on September 13 was made to the 8th Army and the X Army Corps at the northern limits of the city of Lodz. Keitel was a fixture on all of these visits to the front.

The military situation in the command car of the *"Führer"* train was monitored by *Generaloberst* Keitel, head of the *Wehrmachtführungsamt*, *Generalmajor* Jodl who each had a liaison officer for the *Wehrmacht*. Jodl received two daily reports from the Home Defense section under *Oberst d.G.* Warlimont whose section remained in Berlin. The daily Armed Forces bulletin was prepared and released by *Oberst i.G.* Wedel of the *Abteilung Wehrmacht-Propaganda (WPr)* also in Berlin, and this was sent by teletype to the train for Hitler's approval before public release.

Hitler and von Ribbentrop sitting beside the *Sonderzug* in Silesia on September 12.

General Jodl inside the communications car of the *Sonderzug*.

Hitler and a large column of vehicles visited the front again on September 15 at Jaroslaw where the headquarters of the 14th Army was located and watched the crossing of the San River on a bridge built by German military engineers.

A projected trip to Cracow on September 17 was canceled because of troop movements by Soviet units now moving into eastern Poland. Hitler is shown disembarking his train. Max Wünsche is in the foreground.

Relaxing by the train during a stop. Left to right: Von Bülow, Engel, Bormann and Hitler.

The *Führersonderzug* parked on the railroad line. Hitler is seen walking with *Reichspresschef* Otto Dietrich.

Hitler with members of his military staff.

On September 18, the headquarters transferred to Goddow-Lanz via Lauenberg, arriving at 3:45 PM. The next day Hitler traveled with his entourage to Zoppot where the headquarters was housed in the Hotel Casino. Hitler went to the Danzig harbor and took a naval minesweeper to visit the Westerplatte and the captured Polish defenses there. After the Westerplatte visit (above), Hitler went to Gdingen in the company of Keitel (below).

On September 22nd, Hitler flew by plane to Wyskow where he reviewed the situation of the 3rd Army under its commander, *General der Artillerie* von Küchler. During this visit to the front, Hitler and his entourage inspected a Polish armored train that had been destroyed by Stuka dive bombers.

From left to right: *Generalfeldmarschall* Göring, *General der Flieger* Bodenschatz, liaison officer of the *Luftwaffe* with Hitler, *Generaloberst* Keitel, Hitler, Foreign Minister von Ribbentrop

When the end of the Polish campaign came on September 26th at 9:30 AM, Hitler left Polish
soil in his train, arriving in Berlin at the Stettin station at 5:05 PM. After his return from
Poland, Hitler visited his rooms in the new Chancellery building, The working areas of the
heads of the OKW, the chiefs of the WFA and the various military adjutants were still located
in the old Chancellery, in the Congress Hall. This room served as a map room. Hitler is seen
greeting the CIC German Navy, *Grossadmiral* Raeder. In the background at the map table is
Jodl.

To attend the victory parade in Warsaw, Hitler flew to the Polish capital on October 5th where he took the salute for a 2-1/2 hour parade. Below: Hitler is driven through the streets of Warsaw. Right: Reviewing his troops.

Hitler in his *Sonderzug* near Wassertrüdingen on his way to Munich, June 18, 1940.

From February 1, 1943, Hitler's train was given the code name *"Brandenburg."* The train of the Chief of the OKW had received the name *"Afrika"* earlier and from February 1, 1943 was called *"Braunschweig."* The two trains of the Field Command of the WFSt was originally called *"Atlas"* and later *"Franken I"* and *"Franken II."*

103

# The "*Adlerhorst*" Headquarters

A t the end of October, 1939, Hitler's military adjutants searched for a suitable location for a headquarters in the mid-western section of Germany in the event that the British and French, who had declared war on Germany, would open a campaign. They finally settled on an area in the Taunus mountains near Ziegenberg. The castle and town of Ziegenberg are located 11 kilometers west of Bad Neuheim in a heavily wooded area. Dr. Fritz Todt and Albert Speer were ordered to prepare the area for the new headquarters. Concrete buildings and wooden barracks were constructed and in a cliff area, bunkers were blasted out of the rock. This area was not approved by Hitler because he did not wish to be seen living in a castle.

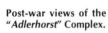

Post-war views of the "*Adlerhorst*" Complex.

The western *Führer* headquarters.

# Field Headquarters "*Felsennest*"
## From May 10 through June 5, 1940

Hitler requested his staff to find another location for his headquarters in the west and an area was finally approved in the rear area zone of the Westwall at Münstereifel. The construction of area "R," later "F" (*Felsennest*) was begun. On the top of a mountain above the village of Rodert the bunker complex was built.. It was heavily camouflaged and concrete bunkers were constructed for Hitler and his staff. In the center of the complex a wooden bunker was erected which served as a map room and living quarters for Jodl's General Staff officer, Deyhle. The barracks in which the daily situation reports were given were heavily camouflaged with thick brush and camouflage nets. (Upper right) The staff of the Home Defense section was located in the vicinity of the village of Rodert in a large farm complex. (Lower right)There was room for about 20 General Staff officers and between 30 to 40 staff assistants

The security units for the *FHQu* were in place towards the end of April, 1940 in the area of Siegburg. When all was in readiness. *Oberstleutnant* Thomas, the commander, gave the code message, "Pentecost holiday approved" to inform Hitler that the headquarters was ready for occupancy. The railroad station at Euskurchen was used for the command train. On May 9, 1940 at 1:00 PM the orders were given in Berlin by *Hauptmann* Engel, Hitler's army adjutant, to begin the move to the new headquarters. A group of the Escort Battalion arrived at the Euskirchen railroad station on May 10th at 12:50 midnight. At 4:25 AM, Hitler's train arrived at the station and at 4:30 AM, his column left for "*Felsennest*," arriving at 5:00 AM.

In his first hour at the new headquarters, Hitler received the news of the capture of the key Belgian fort of Eben Emael by units of the elite German paratroopers.

Hitler's bunker in *"Felsennest."*

Hitler's work room in *"Felsennest."*

Hitler's bedroom in *"Felsennest."*

*FHQu "Felsennest."* See location map on page 105.

Stan Cook

NETHERLANDS

Düsseldorf

0  10  20  30  40
Miles

Cologne

Aachen

Bonn

Bad Münstreifel
Rodert

FHQu "Felsennest"

BELGIUM

Rhine R.

Koblenz

Frankfurt/M.

Mosel R.

Wiesbaden

Main R.

Darmstadt

LUXEMBOURG

Hitler's bunker is heavily camouflaged at *"Felsennest."*

109

In the new headquarters, the daily routine included two daily situation briefings by General Jodl.

Map room in "*Felsennest*"

Situation conference with the CIC Army, *Generaloberst* von Brauchitsch and the Chief of the General Staff, General Halder.

The bunkers in *"Felsennest"* were covered with straw mats as camouflage. 111

Map study in the situation room of the OKW barracks. Left to right: General Jodl, Hitler, Major Willy Deyhle, Jodl's adjutant, and Keitel.

An aerial view of *"Felsennest."*

Hitler on a walk with his naval adjutant, von Putt-kamer.

Hitler and Admiral Raeder at *"Felsennest."*

Hitler and his press chief, Dr. Dietrich.

Hitler walking with his chief military adjutant, Oberst i.G. Schmundt.

On May 24, 1940, Hitler's chief adjutant, Schmundt is conducting a conference with the commanding officer of the headquarters concerning a projected trip of Hitler's to Lille-Armentiers.

Initially projected for May 30-31, this trip was postponed until June 1-2. Flying to Brussels, Hitler took his motorized column through Ypern to Langemarck where he visited the military cemetery from World War I.

Hitler at Langemarck.

On the next morning, Hitler went with his entourage on a round trip through Lille and then to the Vimy heights where he met with the commanding general of the XV Army Corps (motorized), *General der Infanterie* Hoth.

Vestiges of street fighting in Lille.

From left to right: Hoth, Dr. Dietrich, Jodl, Hitler. Behind Hitler, Rommel, then commanding officer of the 7th Panzer Division and Keitel.

# "*Wolfsschlucht*"
## From June 6 through June 26, 1940

With the campaign in the west coming to a conclusion, it was decided to move the headquarters towards the south and on May 19, 1940, the commanding officer of the *FHQu* and Dr. Todt checked over areas east of Avesnes for a suitable site. Later, the commanding officer of the *FHQu*, Schmundt, Engel and Dr. Todt flew to Philipville. In the vicinity of the small town of Brûly-de-Pesche on the French-Belgian border it was decided to establish the new headquarters. The civil population had fled the area. Brûly-de-Pesche was 6 kilometers south west of Couvin in a clearing in the woods. Aside from rebuilding current buildings, a special bunker was built for Hitler, a barracks for him, a mess hall and a barracks for the staff of the Land Defense section. This headquarters was initially called *"Waldwiese."*

Hitler's specially built bunker.

On June 5, 1940, Schmundt indicated that the site was ready for occupancy and by the 6th, the bulk of the staff was in place. Hitler arrived on June 6 at 1:30 PM and changed the name of the camp to *"Wolfsschlucht."*

A wooden barracks had been built for Hitler in the woods (see above) as well as a concrete air raid bunker while his staff was quartered in various local houses (at lower right). Keitel and Jodl were located in the school house as was the map room. The small church served as a casino and a film theater after the altar had been screened with a curtain.

Buildings housing Hitler's Staff.

The school house.

*FHQu "Wolfsschlucht."* See location map on page 105.

Mons

Charleroi

Namur

BELGIUM

FHQu "Wolfsschlucht"
Brûly-de-Pesche

Couvin

Hirson

FRANCE

Charleville-Mézières

Sedan

0   10   20   30

Miles

Stan Cook

Hitler, Bodenschatz, Göring and Bormann in front of the small church.

119

**An aerial view of Brûly-de-Pesche.**

It was in the western campaign of 1940 that Hitler took a significant part in the military leadership.

Hitler, Bodenschatz and Wolff.

Hitler and his closest advisors discussing the successful campaign in the west. Left to right: Dr. Brandt, SS General Wolff, Dr. Morell, Engel, Bodenschatz, Bormann, Dr. Dietrich, Keitel and back to the camera, Jodl.

Hitler and the CIC Army. Left to right: Keitel, Deyhle, Jodl, Hitler, and von Brauchitsch.

Hitler orients his visitor, Rudolf Hess, on the latest battle developments. Also present are Martin Bormann, *Generaloberst* Keitel and at far right, Max Wünsche.

Hitler bids Göring farewell as he is about to board his Fieseler *"Storch"* to return to his headquarters, the special train *"Asien."*

Hitler and Engel after a morning situation report at the *"Wolfsschlucht."*

Walther Hewel of the Foreign Office reports to a relaxing *Führer.*

Hitler reads a report recently given to him at the *"Wolfsschlucht."*

Hitler stomps his foot upon hearing that the French had requested an armistice on June 17, 1940.

# Armistice with France

Through the offices of the Spanish Ambassador in Berlin, the French government sought an armistice with Germany on June 17th. Hitler gave instructions to Keitel and Jodl and the technical details were worked out. Hitler insisted that the ceremony be carried out at Rethondes in the forest of Compiegné, the same location where Germany signed her armistice in 1918.

At noon on June 17, Hitler left the *"Wolfsschlucht"* and flew to Frankfurt/M where he joined his *Sonderzug* (Special Train) for a trip to Munich where he had a scheduled meeting with Mussolini. The train arrived at the Munich station at noon on June 18 and Hitler traveled to the *Führerbau* on the Arcis Street.

Travelling through the streets of Munich on June 18.

In the *Führerbau*.

On the balcony of the *Führerbau*.

Hitler returned to the "*Wolfsschlucht*," leaving Munich on June 19 at 2:15 PM and in the meantime, the WFSt had prepared the terms for the armistice.

To attend the armistice ceremony, Hitler left the "*Wolfsschlucht*" at 3:00 PM and traveled by car to the scene. (above) Here he reviewed units of the Escort Battalion and after the arrival of the French delegation under General Huntzinger, commenced the meeting.

Waiting for the French delegation.

General Keitel is seen reading the terms to the assembled French delegates. They are seated in the same dining car in which the Germans surrendered in 1918.

After the ceremony, Hitler returned to "*Wolfsschlucht.*"

After Hitler's departure, the meeting with the French delegates continued with Keitel, Jodl and *Oberstleutnant d.G.* Böhme and *Hauptmann i.G.* Poleck from the Home Defense section.

The armistice with France was signed at 6:50 PM, June 22, 1940. After the signing, Keitel and the officers from the OKW flew to the "*Wolfsschlucht.*"

The military campaign against France ended on June 25, 1940 at 1.35 AM. At four points of the "*Wolfsschlucht*," hornists of the *Führer-Begleit-Batallion* sounded the call, "Complete halt."

The news of the armistice was broadcast in Germany by a special bulletin. Hitler waited for this in the middle of his entourage.

The special bulletin is aired!

# "Tannenberg"
## From June 27 through July 5, 1940

After the armistice with the French, Hitler's headquarters was transferred from Brûly-de-Pesche in Belgium to "Tannenberg" in the
northern Schwarzwald. This position had been constructed in the
winter of 1939/40. The orders to activate the area came from Hitler's military adjutant on June 26.

The "Tannenberg" quarters lay several kilometers northwest of the
Alexanderschanze on a 1000 meter high mountain, the Kniebis near the
Schwarzwald main highway. It consisted of a few bunkers, blockhouses
and wooden barracks. In Restricted Zone I there was very little spare room
so the immediate members of Hitler's entourage were housed in nearby
guest houses. Hitler's concrete bunker was half-buried in the ground and
the entire compound was surrounded by heavy woods and barbed wire
fences. In the vicinity of the headquarters was a small landing strip for
courier planes. Hitler entered "Tannenberg" on June 28 at 11:00 AM.

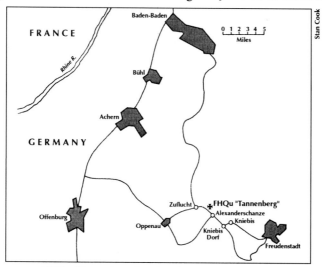

*FHQu "Tannenberg."* **See location map on page 105.**

In the background is the guest house *"Zuflucht"* were the military staff of the WFA was quartered.

On June 29, Hitler inspected the battlefields in the Alsace and visited the cathedral in Strassburg.

Keitel, Hitler and Minister of State Meissner are seen leaving the cathedral (above). Behind Meissner, is *General der Artillerie* Dollmann, Commander of the 7th Army whose units broke through the Maginot Line in Alsace.

From Strassburg, Hitler traveled with his motorized column to Schlettstadt-Colmar and from there to the battlefields in the Vosgen. The return trip of the column went through Breisach (below) Gutach-Wolfach to Kniebis.

On the 30 of June, Hitler traveled by train from Oppenau to Riegel near Freiburg im Briseagu and from there, went with the motorized column to Mühlhausen and into the upper Alsace area where he inspected bunkers of the Maginot Line.

During the trip through the Vosges, Hitler stopped for lunch at a field kitchen. From left to right: Hitler, General Dollmann, Minister Dr. Lammers and Dr. Meissner. With back to the camera is Heinrich Himmler, head of the SS.

Hitler and some of his younger adjutants makes a circuit of the grounds at "Tannenberg."

In the vicinity of "Tannenberg" was a group of female Labor Service personnel who visited him in his headquarters. This was the only group of non-military personnel who ever entered any of his military headquarters during the course of the war.

On July 4, Hitler's Chief Adjutant, Schmundt started the program for the removal of Hitler's headquarters staff to Berlin. The entourage left "Tannenberg" on July 5, arriving the following day at 3:00 PM. Hitler's *Sonderzug* arrived at the Oppenau railroad station on July 4 at 11:00 PM. Before continuing on to Berlin, Hitler made a visit to the military hospital at Freudenstadt and then returned to Oppenau, leaving at 1:00 PM

Hitler arriving at Oppenau.

Hitler's security units left "Tannenberg," transferring to "*Adlerhorst*" at Ziegenberg. Only a small watch detachment remained at "Tannenberg" and this installation was never used again. After the war, American combat engineers blew up the bunkers to prevent the area becoming a tourist attraction.

Traces of the installation at "Tannenberg" can be seen in these postwar photographs.

# Return from the Western Front
## to Berlin

The *Führer* Special Train arrived at the Anhalter railroad station at 3:00 PM on July 6, 1940. Hitler was greeted by the top echelon of his military, Party and government and, outside the station, reviewed an honor company .

Hitler's return to his capital after the brilliantly successful campaign in the west was a great personal triumph for him. The streets of Berlin between the railroad station and the Chancellery on the Wilhelmplatz were packed with cheering Berliners; the streets were covered with flowers and all of the church bells of Berlin rang.

Hitler and his top leadership appeared on the Chancellery balcony before a huge, cheering crowd in the Wilhelmsplatz. Left to right: Göring, Hitler, Raeder, von Brauchitsch, von Ribbentrop and Keitel.

Hitler arrives for a reception commemorating the victory in the west.

# "Berghof"

After a brief stay in Berlin, the *FHQu* was moved to the Berchtesgaden area. Hitler took up quarters in his *Berghof* home while Keitel and Jodl and their adjutants moved into government buildings in the town of Berchtesgaden, The military staff of the Land Defense. units remained in their special train, *"Atlas"* parked on a siding at Bad Reichenhall

On July 17, Hitler met with members of his command staff to discuss the defense of the newly-acquired French coastline and a possible assault on England, *"Operation Seelöwe."*

Left to right: General Jodl, Hitler, Field Marshal Keitel and a naval officer, a representative of the CIC Navy.

The *Berghof.*

The first plans for a possible offensive against Russia was discussed by a staff conference on July 31 at the *Berghof.*

Left to right: Jodl, General Halder, head of the Army General Staff, Hitler, von Brauchitsch and Keitel.

Before the eastern campaign, Hitler met with statesmen of countries that would be allied with Germany on the war with the Soviet Union. On June 6, 1941, Hitler met with the Croatian head of state, Ante Pavelić at the *Berghof.*

To the far right is Albert Bormann, brother of Martin Bormann.

Mussolini visited Hitler at the *Berghof* and on April 29, 1942.

Left to right: Mussolini, Jodl, Hitler, Keitel, *Oberstleutnant d.g.* Christian, General Staff officer of the Luftwaffe with the head of the WFSt, Interpreter Schmidt and Field Marshal Kesselring.

Mussolini and Hitler leave the *Berghof.*

King Boris of Bulgaria was another visitor to the *Berghof*. Below he is seen with Hitler, reviewing a guard of honor of *Waffen-SS* men.

King Boris and Hitler decend the steps of the *Berghof*.

*FHQu "Frühlingssturm."* See location map on page 148.

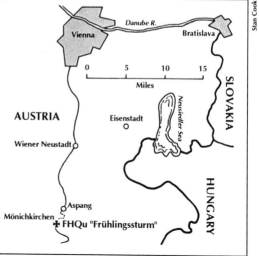

# "*Frühlungssturm*"
## From April 12 through April 25, 1941

On April 6, 1941 at 5:45 AM the offensive against Yugoslavia began. Because this campaign was not planned, there was no time to build a special headquarters so the *Sonderzug* was utilized instead. This train arrived on April 12th at 7:30 AM at Mönichkirchen (about 35 kilometers south of Wiener Neustadt). Because of the possibility of air raids, the train was stopped close to a railroad tunnel. A nearby hotel housed the staff of the Land Defense units.

Hitler's command car was also his work area. Here he received the daily situation reports.   143

Keitel, von Brauchitsch and Hitler.

On April 20, 1941, Hitler celebrated his birthday with a review of the *Führer-Begleit-Bataillon* in the company of his senior military leaders.

*Oberstleutnant* Thomas, commander of the *FHQu,* congratulates Hitler on his birthday.

The *Führersonderzug* at Mönichkirchen in April 1941.

The headquarters remained at Mönichkirchen until April 25. Left to right: Jodl, Hitler, Major von Below, Albert Bormann.

Hitler and Julius Schaub walk next to the *Sonderzug "Amerika"* at Mönichkirchen.

In conversation at the *Führerzug.* From left to right: *Major* Christian, Keitel, Jodl.

On April 26, Hitler made a tour in his car to Graz via Marburg a.d.Douau and on April 27, to Klagenfurt (photo above). He traveled then to Munich on the 28th of April, returning to Berlin.

The entire month of May and the first half of June, 1941, the *FHQu* remained at Berchtesgaden.

Just before the opening of the eastern campaign, Hitler received in Munich the Romanian chief of state, Joan George Antonescu. Hitler came from the *Berghof* to Munich and met Antonescu at the Munich railroad station. They went to the *Führerbau* for a conference. After the conclusion of this meeting, Hitler took his train to Berlin where he arrived on June 13 at 11:40 PM.

Antonescu and Hitler in Munich.

On June 14, a large conference was held in the Reichs Chancellery with all the heads of services, the commanders of Army Groups, Armies, and Panzer Groups where the details of "Barbarossa" were explained.

Location map of the eastern *Führer* headquarters. Note *"Wolfsschanze"* in East Prussia.

# *"Wolfsschanze"*
## From June 24, 1941 through July 15, 1941

I n anticipation of the possibility of a military campaign against the Soviet Union, in October of 1940, a search for a suitable site for a military headquarters was initiated by Hitler through his chief adjutant, Schmundt, his army adjutant Engel and Dr. Fritz Todt.

The site selected was located a few kilometers east of the East Prussian town of Rastenberg. It lay 8 kilometers east of the town in the forest of "Görlitz," owned by the town. This new headquarters was given the name of *"Wolfsschanze"* and it lay on the rail and road system that ran between Rastenberg and Angerberg. One kilometer to the north side of the road and rail right of way was Hitler's area; *Sperrkreis I* and on the southern side

Hitler and his entourage came to the *"Wolfsschanze"* for the first time on June 24th, 1941 at 1:30 AM. (picture on left) Hitler, with Admiral Raeder and other members of his inner circle are seen on a tour of the new facility.

lay *Sperrkreis II* which housed the military staffs of the WFSt, the commander of the camp, a casino and courier center. In *Sperrkreis I* was located Hitler's personal quarters with his air raid bunker, the bunkers of Keitel, Dr. Dietrich, Bormann and the headquarters signal central as well as the quarters of Jodl, Göring and individuals connected with the *Wehrmachtadjutantur*. The headquarters lay in a heavily wooded area and the buildings were built in the cover of the trees and draped with camouflage netting. In the beginning, the headquarters were housed in 8 wooden buildings, built above ground. Later, the headquarters were extensively enlarged and the buildings were sheathed in concrete.

The military situations conferences were held, until July of 1942 in the map room of the head of the WFSt, General Jodl. As previously, Jodl conducted these conferences on a twice-daily basis. The so-called mid-day conference began at 1:00 PM and the evening conference usually ran from between 11:00 PM and 1:00AM.

The barracks of General Jodl.

General of Artillery Alfred Jodl.

Dining room in the "*Wolfsschanze*" On the wall was a red star cut from a downed Soviet aircraft but it was soon removed at Hitler's request.

Hitler before the conference bunker with Keitel. To the left, Dr. Dietrich.

Hitler greeting Heinrich Himmler, head of the SS. Left of Himmler, General Jodl.

The registration table at the *"Wolfsschanze."*

Insects were a problem at Rastenburg.

The Telex room at the *"Wolfsschanze."*

Hitler inspects his new headquarters in June 1941.

The mailroom.

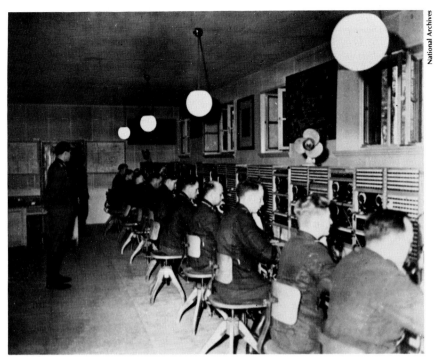

The "*Wolfsschanze*" telephone exchange.

The teletype office.

Above left: Hitler's dining room. Above: The barber shop at the *"Wolfsschanze."* Hitler personally requested that Ernst Wollenhaupt, head barber at the Kaiserhof Hotel in Berlin, be put in charge of this shop.

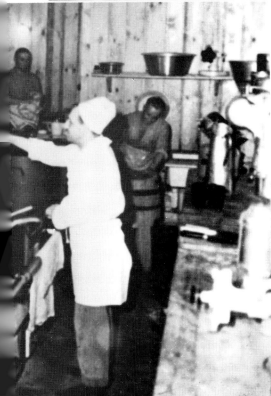

Left: The kitchen area for Hitler's personal staff members.

157

Hitler's office.

The *Führer's* private sitting room where he entertained guests.

Part of Hitler's personal complex.

This cozy room was adjacent to the area shown above.

The *"Wolfsschanze"* sauna room.

A typical office in the headquarters.

Duty office of an LAH NCO.

An interior corridor in the complex.

The CIC Army, Field Marshal von Brauchitsch with his adjutant *Oberstleutnant* von Gyldenfeldt and Hitler's Chief Adjutant, Schmundt.

On the 25th of August, 1941, Mussolini arrived at the "*Wolfsschanze*" in his special train at 11:00 AM for a conference with Hitler. At the Görlitz rail road station with Hitler to greet Mussolini were Foreign Minister von Ribbentrop, Keitel, Bormann and Jodl. After a tour of the headquarters, a high-level conference was held in the situation bunker.

Hitler personally greets Mussolini as he arrives by train.

After the conference.

Hitler and Mussolini flew on August 26th from the airfield at Rastenberg to Terespol in Russia, west of Brest. There they were hosted by Field Marshals von Bock, von Kluge and Kesselring and given a tour of the captured fortress of Brest.

Hitler and Mussolini at the Rastenburg airfield.

**At Terespol.**

**Approaching the captured fortress of Brest.**

In the evening, Hitler and Mussolini traveled in their special trains to Camp "South" near Krasno where they arrived on August 27th at 5:00 PM. This camp consisted merely of a railroad tunnel and several wooden barracks.

*Generaloberst* Löhr and *Generalfeldmarschall* von Rundstedt join Mussolini and Hitler in the Ukraine on August 28.

The communications section of the *FHQu* was responsible for telephone, telegraph and teletype communications and was initially a platoon strength. In 1943 this was enlarged to a section. It was initially called *Nachrichten-Abteilung zbv 3* or Signals Section for Special Use 3. It was initially under the command of *Oberst* Sander, later *Hauptmann* Kleckel. The commanding officer of the entire section was *Major* Wolf.

Quarters of the staff of the Signals Company of the FHQ in the winter of 1941/42.

Room of a NCO in the personnel barracks of the Signals Section, *FHQu*, 1944.

For the Finnish troops who fought alongside the Germans on the east front, Hitler awarded the Finnish Field Marshal von Mannerheim the Knight's Cross on August 8, 1941. It was officially presented to him by *Gen. d. Art.* Jodl on September 4.

The Regent of Hungary, Admiral Horthy, arrived at the *FHQu* in his special train on September 8, 1941 and participated in the daily conference. A projected visit to the front had to be canceled because the Admiral refused to fly.

National Archives

Horthy after his arrival at "*Wolfsschanze*" in conversation with von Ribbentrop, Keitel and Bormann.

Hitler and von Ribbentrop greet President Josef Tiso and Dr. Tuka (in background) from Slovakia on October 20, 1941.

King Boris of Bulgaria arrived at the "*Wolfsschanze*" in his special train on March 24, 1942, at 11:00 AM. At the railroad station he was greeted by von Ribbentrop, Keitel, Bormann and Jodl.

King Boris and Hitler at the "*Wolfsschanze*."

*Grossadmiral* Dr. h.c. Raeder and Foreign Minister von Ribbentrop.

*Reichsministers* Graf Schwerin-Krosigk, Dr. Goebbels and Dr. Frick.

*Reichsministers* Speer and Rosenberg, and *Reichskommissar* Dr. Seyss-Inquart.

On April 26, 1942 Hitler addressed a meeting of the *Reichstag.*

Accompanied by Keitel, Schmundt, *Generalmajor* Heusinger and *Oberst* Scherff, Hitler flew on June 1, 1942 to visit Army Group South near Poltava where he conferred with the military commanders involved in the battle of Kharkov.

Arriving at the conference near Poltava.

Hitler conferences concerning the campaigns of the summer of 1942.

Hitler flew to Finland to make a short visit to Field Marshal von Mannerheim on the latter's 75th birthday in June of 1942. Hitler was accompanied by Keitel, Ambassador Hewel and Dr. Dietrich. On this flight, one of the tires on his special Fw 200 caught fire as the landing gear was retracted but the fire went out and there was no damage to the aircraft.

Hitler, Keitel and von Mannerheim.

Hitler greets members of von Mannerheim's staff.

On June 27, 1942, von Mannerheim made another visit to Hitler. He was received at the airfield by Keitel and Jodl, reviewed an honor guard of the Escort Battalion and was then taken to see Hitler.

National Archives

In *"Sperrkreis I"* von Mannerheim took part in the daily briefing conference.

National Archives

The Rumanian head of state and CIC of the Rumanian Army, Marshal Antonescu made a number of trips to the *FHQu*. He participated in the daily conferences, escorted by General Jodl.

# "Wehrwolf"
## From July 16 through October 30, 1942

I n the middle of 1942, it was decided to move the *Führer* headquarters to an area in the Ukraine so that Hitler could more closely observe the progress of Army Group South. On July 16, the *FHQu* moved to the area of Vinnitsa in the Ukraine. The camp itself was located in the woods, 15 kilometers north east of Vinnizia on the road to Zhitomir. This camp consisted of blockhouses and concrete bunkers and was given the name of *"Wehrwolf"* by Hitler. Sperrkreise I & II were within a hundred meters of each other and the entire headquarters was surrounded with high wire fences and guarded by the Escort Battalion.

In the new headquarters, July, 1942. Left to right: Schulze-Kossens, Hitler Junge, Schmundt, von Puttkamer.

*SA-Chef* Viktor Lutze (far right) visited the *"Wehrwolf"* complex from July 24-28, 1942.

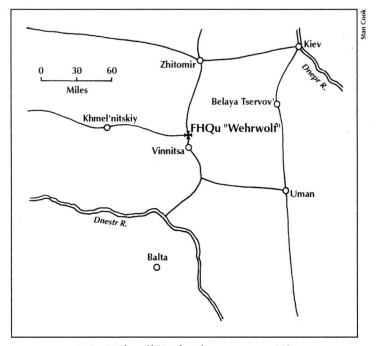

*FHQu "Wehrwolf."* See location map on page 148.

In the Casino of *"Wehrwolf"* on September 20, 1942. The birthday of Hitler's *Luftwaffe* Adjutant, *Major* von Below. From left to right: Albert Bormann, Julius Schaub, *Kapitän zur See* von Puttkamer, *Major* Engel, *SS-Hauptsturmführer* Schulze-Kossens, Johanna Wolf (Hitler's secretary) and *Major* von Below.

In September of 1942, there was a serious breach between Hitler and Jodl over the situation in the Caucaus. Following this, the daily situation conference was no longer held in Jodl's quarters but in Hitler's and Hitler stopped eating in the officer's mess. It was at this point that stenographers were brought in to record all of the conferences. Hitler claimed that his verbal instructions were being misinterpreted. The only officer in the OKW that Hitler dealt with was his Chief Adjutant, General Schumudt.

General Jodl acted as an effective liaison between the commanders at the front and the High Command. Here is seen in conversation with the CIC South, Field Marshal Albert Kesselring.

Hitler and General Schmundt.

Croat leader Dr. Ante Pavelić visits Hitler at *"Wehrwolf."*

Construction style at *"Wehrwolf."*

Entrance to an underground Bunker.

The swimming pool.

# Back to "*Wolfsschanze*"
## From October 31, 1942 through November 20, 1944

On October 31, 1942, Hitler and his command returned to "*Wolfsschanze*" and on November 7, Hitler, Keitel and Jodl went by train to Munich and on November 14, to Berchtesgaden. Hitler took up residence in the *Berghof* and Jodl and Keitel occupied quarters in the "Little Chancellery" in Berchtesgaden. The WFSt units that had remained in "*Wolfsschanze*" moved to Salzburg on November 21 and were quartered later in the Mountain troops barracks in Strup near Berchtesgaden. Because of the worsening military situation, the *FHQu* returned to "*Wolfsschanze*" between November 23 and 25.

National Archives

In the *"Wolfsschanze"* Hitler held a conference on December 19 with the Italian Foreign Minister, Count Ciano and the French head of state, Pierre Laval. This picture was taken in the map room of the *FHQu* where the daily situation reports were given. Left to right: Schmidt (translator), Laval, Hitler, Ciano, Göring, foreground, von Ribbentrop.

In January, 1943, Hitler received the Bulgarian War Minister Lieutenant General Michoff.

Dr. Schmidt, Marshal Antonescu and Hitler at "*Wolfsschanze*" on February 13.

Antonescu is given a tour of the Rastenburg communications center.

From February 17 through the 19, Hitler went with Generals Jodl and Zeitzler, Chief of the Army General Staff, to the headquarters of Army Group South at Saparohshje. Here, Hitler ordered the recapture of the entire Donez area and the city of Kharkov.

Hitler in conference at the headquarters of Army Group South where he ordered the recapture of the Donez area.

Hitler then went to *"Wehrwolf"* near Vinnizia where he remained until March 13.

Hitler celebrates his 54th birthday at the Obersalzburg.

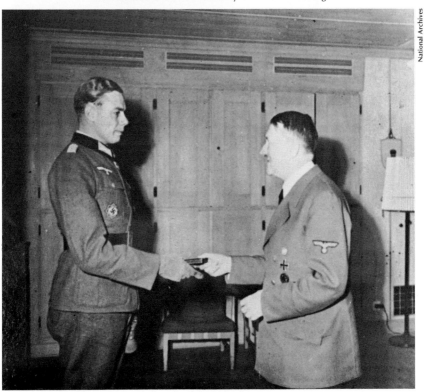

Erich Bärenfänger receives his Oakleaves to the Knight's Cross on May 17.

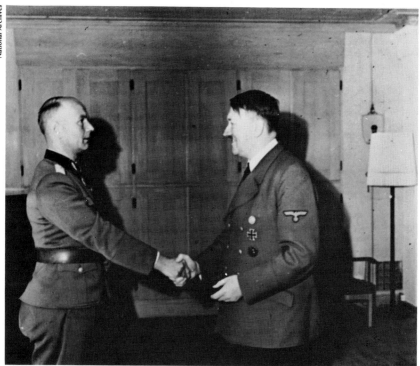

Otto Kumm is awarded his Oakleaves in May.

Hitler presents Speer with the Fritz Todt honor ring in June, 1943.

Adalbert Schulz receives his Swords in August, 1943.

In early August Helmut Lent receives his Swords, and Egmont Prinz zur Lippe-Weissenfeld, Manfred Meuer, Joachim Kirschner, and Heinrich Ehrler receive their Oakleaves.

Walter Krüger receives his Oakleaves on August 31.

Waiting for Mussolini after his rescue from captivity on September 12.

Mussolini arrives at Rastenburg airfield on September 15, 1943. He had been in Munich until his flight.

189

Skorzeny who accompanied Mussolini, meets privately with Hitler.

Kaltenbrunner, Hitler and Skorzeny walk to the conference room at the *"Wolfsschanze."*

Paul Schultz, Dr. Walter Lange, Theodor Tolsdorff, Günther Pape and Dr. Franz Bäke receive their Oakleaves in late September.

In late September Hartmann Grasser and Heinrich Prinz zu Sayn-Wittgenstein receive their Oakleaves, and Günter Rall and Walter Nowotny their Swords.

Emilio Esteban-Infantes, commander of the Spanish "Blue Division" receives his Knight's Cross at the "*Wolfsschanze*" on October 3.

Hitler greets Party leaders at the "*Wolfsschanze*" on October 10, 1943. From left to right: *Gauleiter*s Jordan, Eigruber, von Schirach, Murr, Spenger, Hitler, Weinrich, Schwede-Coburg, Himmler, Rosenberg, ?, ?, and Schwarz.

Hitler speaks to Party members at the *"Löwenbräukeller"* in Munich on November 9.

Hitler presents the Oakleaves to Hasso von Manteuffel, Ernst Wellmann, Willi Langkeit, and Karl Baacke in late December 1943 at the "*Wolfsschanze.*"

In mid-January 1944 Albert v.d. Goltz, Karl Koetz, Josef-Georg Mulzer, and Andreas Thorey are awarded their Oakleaves.

Theo-Helmut Lieb receives his Knight's Cross on February 7, 1944.

Hitler awards the Knight's Cross of the War Merit Cross to Theo Morell, his personal physician, on February 24, 1944.

Hitler meets with the ranking officers from the western front at *Schloss* Klessheim on March 20, 1944. Rommel is second from left.

Hitler accompanies Mussolini as he greets a wounded Italian officer on April 25, 1944.

The last building projects at "Wolfsschanze" began in March of 1944. As protection against air attack, the buildings were encased in massive concrete shells and new concrete bunkers were constructed. The "*Führerbunker*" shown below had a thickness of 7 meters of concrete.

At the same event the new 8.8cm Pak 43 on a cruciform mount is inspected.

On April 20, 1944 Hitler was in the Klessheim area where he reviewed new weaponry. Left: Keitel, Hitler, Göring and Karl Otto Saur (department head of the Armaments Ministry) inspect the new "*Hetzer*" tank killer. Below: Hitler views a column of "*Hetzers*" as they roll past on a nearby *Autobahn*.

## The 7.5cm Pak 40/4L on Chassis *"Raupenschlepper Ost."*

An experimental 88mm gun.

National Archives

National Archives

A prototype of the *"Sturmmörsertiger"* (Assault Tiger).

On May 12 Hitler met with Dr. Tiso and other Slovakian leaders at *Schloss* Klessheim.

On June 3, 1944 Hitler attended the wedding of Hermann Fegelein and Gretl Braun. Himmler and Bormann were best men.

202

One June 6, 1944 Hitler was roused from bed at Berchtesgaden and given the news of the Normandy invasion. He was then driven to *Schloss* Klessheim where he conducted a conference with his staff. They are shown studying a map of northern France.

Because of the construction at "*Wolfsschanze*," the entire *FHQu* was removed to the Berchtesgaden area in the middle of March. From here, Hitler flew on June 17 in the company of Jodl and Schmundt to the west and stayed in the "*Wolfsschlucht II*" area where he met with Field Marshals Rommel and von Rundstedt. This headquarters lay 8 kilometers north east of Soissons in a deep railroad cutting with one concrete bunker (below), wooden bunkers and a tunnel in which the special train was parked. Hitler was at "*Wolfsschlucht II*" for only one day.

Because of the situation in the east, Hitler did not wait for completion of the construction at "*Wolfsschanze*" but returned to his eastern headquarters on July 14 after a brief stop in Berchtesgaden.

Hitler is welcomed back to his eastern headquarters. Keitel and Dönitz are directly behind Hitler.

National Archives

At the "*Wolfsschanze*" on July 15, 1944. From left to right: von Stauffenberg, von Puttkamer, Bodenschatz (back to camera), Hitler and Keitel. Note the pole construction for suspension of camouflage netting.

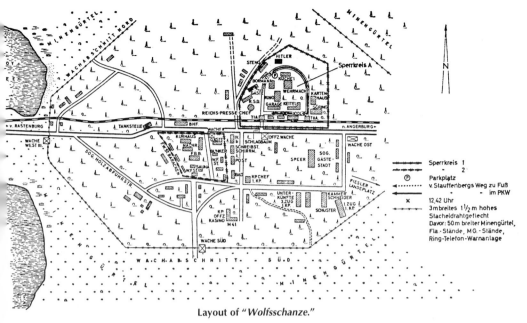

Layout of "Wolfsschanze."

July 20, 1944 was a very hot summer day. The daily situation conference was held in a wooden barracks that generally was used by visitors. At 12:45 PM, a bomb planted by *Oberst* Graf v. Stauffenberg in a briefcase, exploded. The situation room was badly damaged (below) but Hitler survived with only minor injuries.

Immediately after hearing of the assassination attempt, political leaders rush to give well wishes to the *Führer.* Note Hitler greets them with his left hand as his right one had been injured.

Göring, Himmler and Hitler.

Hitler and Goebbels.

Hitler and Lammers.

Himmler, Hitler and Fegelein.

Above: Fegelein's breeches.

Left: Hitler's trousers.

Hitler, Goebbels and Kaltenbrunner.

Hitler and his entourage have just viewed the damage at the *Lagezimmer.*

A short time after the attempt, Hitler allowed himself to be photographed with his advisors. Left to right: Keitel, Göring, Hitler, Bormann and Himmler. Behind Hitler, Günsche, Jodl (with head bandage) and von Below.

In the evening of July 20-21, Hitler, Göring and *Grossadmiral* Dönitz spoke to the German people on the state radio system. Standing against the wall is *Oberstleutnant* Sander, Hitler's Signals officer.

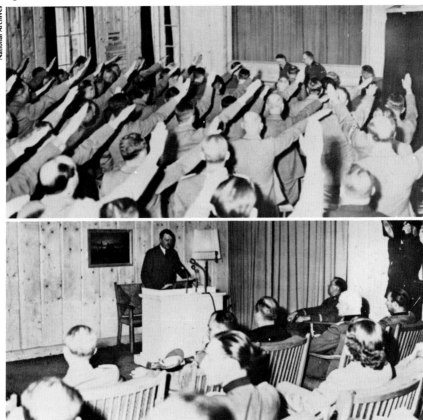

Bormann, Dietrich, Hitler and Schaub are shown waiting for the arrival of Mussolini, who had been scheduled to arrive at Rastenburg on this historic day.

Below: Hitler greets Mussolini after his arrival at the Görlitz railway station.

B. Kudlička

Schaub, Hitler, *Luftwaffe* General Loerzer, Himmler, Mussolini, and Göring walk northward in *Sperrkreis I* (Restricted Zone I), having just left the *Führersperrkreis.*

Mussolini is greeted by Himmler, Wolff and Schaub.

Mussolini is shown the blast damage to the *Lagezimmer.*

Mussolini, Bormann, Dönitz, Hitler, Göring, Fegelein and Loerzer.

After the July 20 bomb blast, Hitler visited all of his wounded staff members on several occasions.

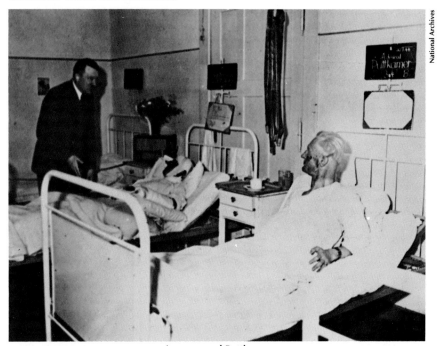

Assmann and Puttkamer.

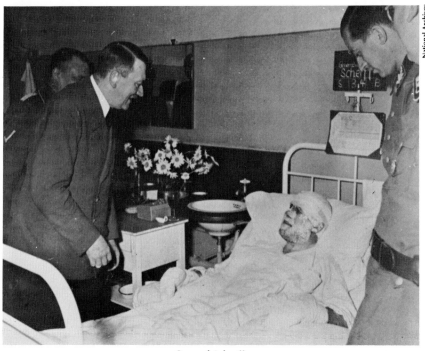

General Scherff.

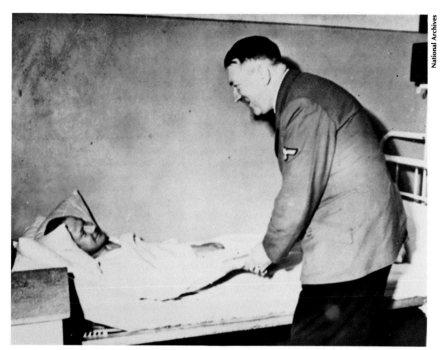

Borgmann.

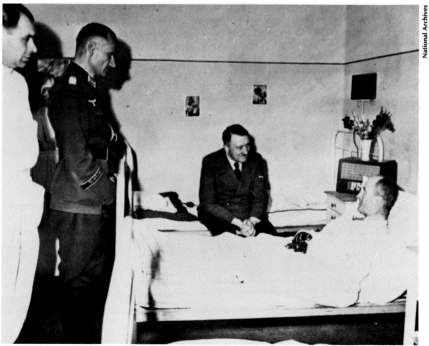

A return visit after Assmann's bandages had been removed. 215

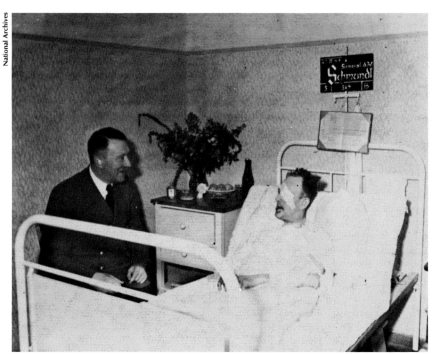

Hitler talks with his critically wounded, chief adjutant Rudolf Schmundt. He later died from his injuries on October 1, 1944.

As Hitler leaves the hospital in Rastenburg he is met by loyal followers.

On August 3 *Reich-* and *Gauleiters* came to the *"Wolfsschanze"* to show their support for their *Führer*. From left to right: Hitler, Himmler, Ley, Dr. Goebbels, Max Amann and Dr. Frick.

During the above event Hitler shakes hands with *SA-Stabschef* Wilhelm Schepmann.

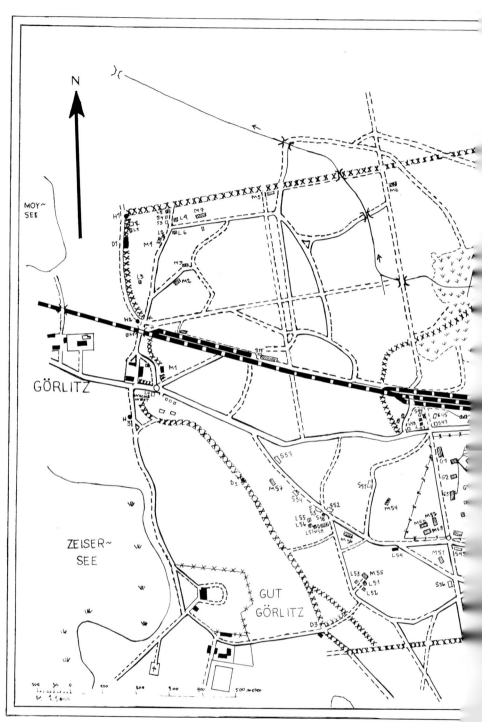

Layout of the "*Wolfsschanze*" and the surrounding area as of August 1, 1944. (From the KTB of the FBB.)

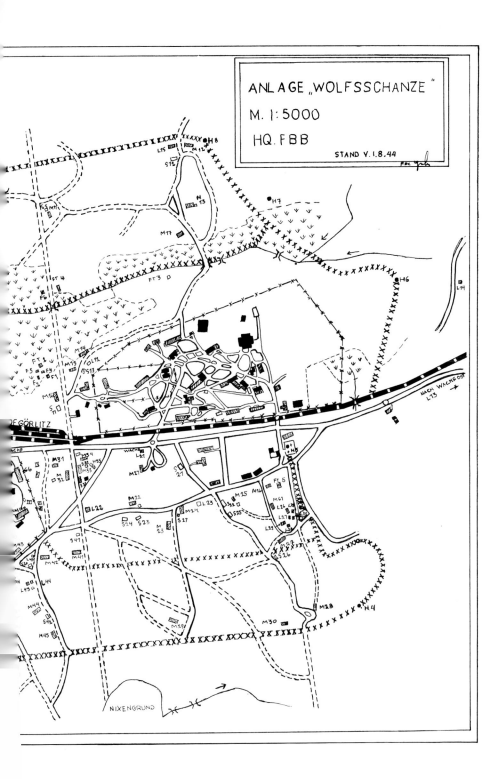

ANLAGE „WOLFSSCHANZE"

M. 1:5000

HQ. FBB

STAND V. 1.8.44

August, 1944, Generals von Manteufel (right) and von Knobelsdorff reported to Hitler in the "*Wolfsschanze.*"

Franz von Papen, Germany's Ambassador to Turkey, is awarded the Knight's Cross of the War Merit Cross on August 19.

Hitler personally awards the Gold Close Combat Clasp on September 5, 1944. This was the second awarding ceremony.

Hitler awards the Gold Close Combat Clasp to Hermann Wulf, Karl Weiss, Wilhelm Loos, Erich Carl and Kurt Rätzel on September 14, 1944. This was the third awarding of the decoration.

*Generaloberst* Heinz Guderian is called to the "*Wolfsschanze*" on September 25, 1944. He is shown meeting with Hitler and Fegelein.

*SS-Obergruppenführer* Hans Jüttner, head of the SS Main Office is awarded the Knight's Cross of the War Merit Cross with Swords on October 30, 1944.

The Russian offensive in October of 1944 reached the borders of East Prussia and the *FHQu* moved on November 20, 1944 to Berlin. To prevent the complex from falling intact into Russian hands, General of Engineers Jacob blew up all the buildings at the beginning of January, 1945. The code name for this destruction was *"Inselsprung."* (The opposite pictures were taken after the war)

# "Wiesental"

## From December 10, 1944 through January 15, 1945.

The WFSt worked since the summer of 1944 on the preparations for a large German counteroffensive in the Ardennes. Hitler moved to Ziegenberg. His staff was at *"Adlerhorst"* and Hitler and his staff were quartered at "Wiesental," about 2 kilometers distant from Ziegenberg. This installation consisted of houses and underground bunkers and was heavily camouflaged by trees and nets.

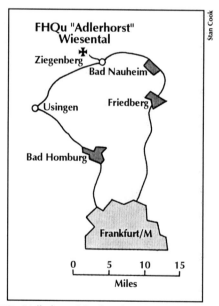

*FHQu "Adlerhorst."* See location map on page 105.

On New Year's morning, 1945, Hitler received congratulations from his staff (above) and on the same day, presented *Oberstleutnant* Hans-Ulrich Rudel the Gold Oakleaves with Swords and Diamonds to the Knight's Cross.

# Berlin Reichs Chancellery
## From January 16, 1945 to May 1945

W ith the beginning of the Soviet offensive against the eastern areas of Germany, Hitler returned to Berlin on January 16, 1945. Here, he established his headquarters in the Reichs Chancellery, and Keitel and Jodl moved their OKW headquarters to Berlin-Dahlem. The field command of the WFSt, which had been situated in a barracks in Friedberg/Hessen while Hitler resided in the west, was now in the camp "Maybach I" near Zossen. After the Chancellery had been heavily damaged by air attacks, Hitler withdrew to the bunker below it.

On February 24, 1945 Hitler awards Konstantin Hierl on his 70th birthday with the Gold Cross of the German Order with Oakleaves and Swords.

On March 11, 1945 Hitler held a conference with the staff of the 9th Army at Bad Saarow on the Scharmüzelsee. Hitler in conversation with CIC 9th Army, General Busse. To Hitler's right, *Generaloberst* Ritter von Greim, the last CIC *Luftwaffe*.

Hitler left his bunker under the Chancellery garden only once, on March 20, 1945, when he decorated members of the Hitler Youth in the Chancellery garden area.

The bunker entrance.

1. Hitler's bedroom.
2. Hitler's living room.
3. Conference room.
4. Anteroom to Hitler's quarters.
5. Eva Braun's bedsitting room.
6. Heating installation.
7. Telephone exchange.
8. Martin Bormann's study.
9. Dr. Josef Goebbels' study.
10. Orderly officers' room.
11. Room of valet, Heinz Linge.

12. Goebbels' bedroom.
13. Waiting room.
14. Guards' room.
15. Observation tower with emergency exit.
16. Exit to the Reich Chancellery garden.

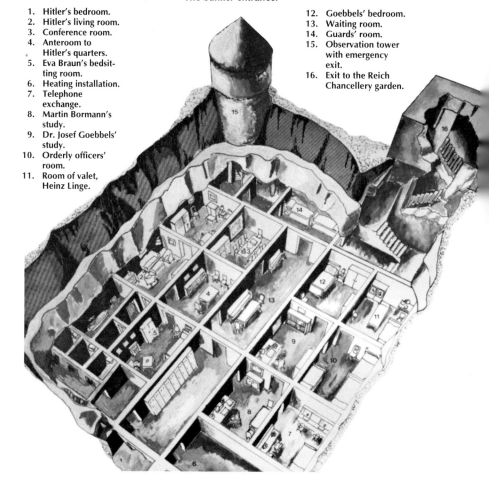

The Reichs Chancellery shortly after the war.

The ruins of the Reichs Chancellery, Hitler's last command post. In front of the buildings in the background was the ventilation tower (right) and the bunker entrance, (left.)

# The Führer-Begleit-Bataillon (Hitler's Military Escort Battalion)

T he *Wach Regiment* or Guard Regiment, of Berlin was instituted on June 23, 1937 and supplied units that served as guards at various significant governmental buildings, including the *Reichskanzelei* or Reich's Chancellery.

One June 12, 1939, this regiment was renamed *Infanterie-Regiment-Grossdeutschland* and on September 25, 1939, immediately after the outbreak of the war with Poland, the *Wach Kompanie* or Guard Company, *Führer-Hauptquartier* was established. On October 1, 1939, this company was expanded to the *Führer-Begleit-Bataillon, FHQu.*

The Army guard detail for Hitler had its genesis in the special unit called the *Führer-Reise* or trip, and originally was intended to protect Hitler on his journeys into newly-acquired German territory in what had been Austria, and the Sudeten area of Czechoslovakia.

In August of 1939, two motorized platoons were formed from the 7th and 8th companies of the Watch Regiment and were officially termed *Mil.Stab des Führers.*

This unit was equipped with VW *Kubelwagen* and *Opel-Blitz* light vehicles and placed under the command of *Oberst* or Colonel, Erwin Rommel, formerly the commanding officer of the *Kriegsschule* or Military School, located at Wiener-Neustadt outside of Vienna in the Ostmark.

This *Führer-Begleit Kommando* or Escort Command, comprised two platoons. The 1st Platoon was taken from the 7th Company of the Watch Regiment and was under the command of *Leutnant* Schneider and the II Platoon taken from the 8th Company was under *Leutnant* Rössler. The senior NCO was *Hauptfeldwebel* Schöttler.

By the end of the month, the unit was enlarged in the Sudeten to include a *Panzer-Abwehr* (anti-tank) platoon armed with the 37 mm anti-tank gun; a 20 mm Flak (anti-aircraft) platoon armed with four-barreled anti-aircraft guns; an armored reconnaissance platoon and a railroad anti-aircraft platoon also armed the same 20 cm guns and assigned to the *Führersonderzug* or Hitler's personal train.

Hitler discusses the military situation during the Polish campaign with Erwin Rommel, commander of the *Führer's* escort unit.

This entire unit was then put under the command of Major von Rohden and Rommel was made the commander of the *Führer-Hauptquartier.*

On August 24,1939 the Rössert Platoon (2nd Platoon) traveled to Stettin and then to Bad Polzin. They took over the protection of Hitler's *Sonderzug* (Special Train) in Gross-Born where Hitler's train was parked during the opening phases of the campaign in Poland.

The mission of the *Führer-Begleit-Kommando* was to guard and secure Hitler's *Sonderzug* (Special Train) and his headquarters and to guard and secure Hitler's person during his trips to the front lines.

At this period, members of the unit wore an armband with the gilt Gothic lettering *"Führerhauptquartier"* on black on their lower left sleeve. In general, this cufftitle was only to be worn inside the headquarters and not in combat situations.

After a brief stay in Berlin, the Commando moved to Lauenberg in Pomerania. In the interim, the command of the unit again reverted to Colonel Rommel.

On September 21, 1939, part of the *Begleit-Kommando* went to Zoppot in the Danzig area and was quartered in the Hotel Victoria. Hitler himself and his headquarters staff were quartered in the Casino-Hotel.

On September 25, 1939, the *Führer-Begleit-Kommando* returned to Berlin, this time not as a part of the *Grossdeutschland* units but as a separate entity and was assigned to the Hermann-Göring barracks in Berlin-Reineckendorf.

The unit was then enlarged and added a Watch Company under the command of *Hauptmann* Kolbeck from the War College in Vienna. Another platoon was formed under the command of *Leutnant* Kraussold.

On October 3, 1939 Hitler presented the unit with its own colors, a red silk standard with a copy of his personal standard on one side and the insignia for the regular Army unit standards on the other.

When the campaign in France began on May 10, 1940, Hitler and his staff moved to the newly-constructed headquarters at *"Felsennest"* near Münstereifel.

On his visits to the front, he was accompanied by units of the Commando and they accompanied him on his trip on June 6 to Dinant.

Members of the *Führer-Begleit-Kommando* were always close to Hitler.

Several days later, the First Guard Company *(1. Wachkompanie)* under the command of *Rittmeister* von Blomberg with platoon leader *Leutnant* Grundmann traveled to Compiégne where, on June 22, 1940, Hitler accepted the surrender of the French forces in the same railroad coach used by the French command in 1918 to accept the surrender of the German Army.

After this ceremony, Hitler went on the same day to Freudenstadt in the Schwarzwald to visit wounded German soldiers in a military hospital.

From July 5, 1940, the Guard Company of the Escort Battalion was stationed at the headquarters complex, *"Adlerhorst"* near Zweigenberg in the state of Hesse. From this point, there were a number of visits to former combat areas.

On October 7, 1940, members of the Escort Battalion received the *"Grossdeutschland"* cufftitle, silver embroidery of the unit name for officers and grey silk thread for enlisted personnel. This title was worn on the lower right sleeve. Also, the unit wore the "GD" cyphers on their shoulder boards.

On October 20, 1940, a detachment of the Escort Battalion motored across France to the Spanish border and the town of Hendeye where Hitler was slated to meet with General Franco, Spanish head of state.

The 2nd Guard Company, called the rapid company, a motorcycle unit, moved to Paris for Hitler's visit to the French capital.

At the beginning of 1941, the bulk of the *Führer-Begleit-Bataillon* was located at Döberitz in the vicinity of Berlin. When there was a lull in the war, Hitler kept his headquarters in the German capital.

As of January 1, 1941, the Battalion was organized as follows:
Staff Company
1st. (Guard) Company commanded by *Hauptmann* Gruss,
2nd (motorized) Company commanded by *Hauptmann* Freiherr von Blomberg,
3rd (heavy weapons) Company commanded by *Hauptmann* Nehring
And one unit that was stationed in field tents.

The commander of the battalion at this time was *Oberstleutnant* Thomas who was under the commander of the *Führerhauptquartier.*

Because the 1st Company was considered a rifle company with a heavy machine gun group as their heaviest weapons, the 2nd Company was more heavily armed with armored reconnaissance cars under the command of *Leutnant* Guderian, a son of Colonel General Guderian. The 3rd Company had anti-aircraft weapons and 50mm anti tank guns and infantry guns.

On January 15, 1941, the Battalion received a new cufftitle *"Führer-hauptquartier"* which replaced the earlier one. This issue had silver, or grey silk embroidery, in German script and was worn on the lower left arm but only outside of the actual headquarters itself.

In March of 1941, the Battalion was strengthened by the addition of the mixed *Flak* Battery "Hermann Göring" under the command of *Hauptmann* Gasda. This unit was equipped with heavy and light anti aircraft weapons. Also added to the original unit was a 4th Company, a tank platoon equipped with Czech PzKw 38 Skoda tanks under the command of *Oberleutnant* Peiper, and a *Führer-Flugzug-Staffel* (or Aircraft unit) for special courier service. Hitler's personal aircraft were attached to this unit. The Battalion also received a *Führer-Nachrichten-Kompanie* or signals section who were responsible for all signals connections outside of the main headquarters.

On April 9, 1941, the bulk of the *Führer-Begleit-Bataillon* was transferred to the command center, *"Frühlingssturm"* in the vicinity of Mönichkirchen in the Steirmark. This was the headquarters used by Hitler during the Yugoslavian campaign.

The *Führer-Begleit-Bataillon* at Mönichkirchen.

This headquarters was located near the Aspang railroad tunnel, 100 meters long and both Hitler's *Sonderzug, "Amerika"* and the train for the High Command of the Armed Forces were attached to engines who always kept steam up in the event that a possible air raid compelled them to seek shelter in the tunnel.

Hitler's train consisted of: two locomotives, a special anti-aircraft car armed with two four-barreled 20-mm guns (on occasions two such cars), manned by a 26 man *Luftwaffe* crew, combination baggage and auxiliary power car, Hitler's personal sleeping car (no. 10206) that also housed his *Wehrmacht* Chief Adjutant, Colonel Schmundt, his chief personal adjutant

This "Hermann Göring" member was assigned to the *Führerhauptquartier*. He was a qualified driver, an aircraft technician and a pilot. He is wearing the cufftitle in German script introduced in January 1941.

and Heinz Linge, his valet. There was also a staff conference car that was equipped with a communications staff, radios and telephones that could be activated at various stops, a special personnel car for his RSD men with a compliment of 22 men, a dining car, a bath and shower car, two additional sleeping cars for members of his staff and occasional guests, two cars for headquarters personnel, a special car equipped as another communications center for Press Chief Otto Dietrich, another baggage and generator car and a second anti-aircraft car.

When Hitler was located at his main wartime headquarters at Rastenburg in East Prussia, this train was parked, under steam, on a camouflaged siding near the Görlitz railroad station and when in Berlin, at the Tempelhof depot.

While still at *"Frühlungssturm,"* Hitler celebrated his 52 birthday on April 20, 1941 by reviewing the men of the Escort Battalion accompanied by *Reichsmarschall* Göring, *Reichsführer-SS* Himmler and other high-ranking officials.

Following the successful conclusion of the Yugoslavian campaign, *"Amerika"* departed *"Frühlingssturm"* at 2:00 AM, April 26, for southern Austria and the province of Carinthia, returning to Berlin on April 28.

Units of the Escort Battalion and members of the *Organization Todt,* the special construction service, went to Rastenberg and began to construct a military headquarters in the State Forest of Rastenberg, east of the town, in preparation for the forthcoming campaign against the Soviet Union.

On the evening of the 19th through the 20th of June, the greatly strengthened *Führer-Begleit-Bataillon* departed their Berlin base at Döberitz for the new headquarters, *"Wolfsschanze."*

The new Armor Company which accompanied them was commanded by Hauptmann Rohrbeck. The personnel of this unit wore the standard black clothing of all German Panzer units but instead of a pink piping, these men wore white piping as well as both the *Grossdeutschland* and *Führer-Hauptquartier* cufftitles.

The FBB would never again return to Berlin as a unit.

While *Wehrmacht* units were moving into position for their assault on the Soviet Union, the Escort Battalion was moving into the new *Führerhauptquartier (FHQu)* in the vicinity of Rasterberg. Defense positions were prepared in the area of heavy woods and marsh land. Barbed wire fences were erected and the first of many buildings designed to house Hitler's military headquarters were readied for their new occupants.

Hitler's personal quarters were called Haus 11 and was located in Secured Zone One *(Sperrkreis I),* while the other buildings were located in *Sperrkreis II.*

The perimeters were surrounded with high wire fences topped off with barbed wire. Guard towers had been erected along the perimeter that had four entrances; Guard North, South, East and West. The Escort Battalion was housed in wooden barracks while the Panzer Company was initially quartered on the eastern side of the compound. Anti-aircraft units, mainly designed to protect against Soviet paratroop units were installed in towers and on the ground in permanent positions.

Supply and support units were quartered in the small villages in the neighborhood of the compound and motorized units made daily long patrols through the neighboring woods and small lakes.

Battalion members, often in civilian attire, constantly patrolled both the outer perimeters and the inner one that encompassed Hitler's quarters.

The city of Rastenberg was about 5 kilometers to the west of the headquarters and the daily courier train from Berlin used the railroad station there rather than the Görlitz station situated inside the perimeter fencing of the camp..

At Rastenberg was located the barracks of the former Imperial Grenadier Regiment, *"Friedrich der Grosse"* and these were now occupied by reserve units of the Escort Battalion.

Between Rastenberg and the *FHQu* was an improved road and on it were the buildings for a military hospital. When members of the Battalion were injured in the numerous small accidents with motorcycles and other vehicles during their patrols, it was to this hospital that they went for treatment.

To the northeast of the *"Wolfsschanze"* was the *"Mauerwald"* complex that housed the barracks and work area of the Army High Command and to the east, near the small town of Grossgarten was "Hochwald," Himmler's headquarters.

The small airfield that served the camp was located south of Rastenberg and units of the *Führer-Kurier-Staffel* were quartered there.

The entire complex was under the command, in 1941, of *Oberstleutnant* Thomas and his staff was organized as follows:

| | |
|---|---|
| Adjutant: | *Hauptmann Schwerdt* |
| 00 : | *Oberleutnant Seldte* |
| | *Rittmeister von Möllendorf* |
| Ia | *Hauptmann Baum* |
| | *Major Sewald* |
| | *Hauptmann Peiper* |
| IIb | *Leutnant Kratsch* |
| IVb (Construction) | *Oberleutnant Niemeyer* |
| | *Hauptmann Spengemann* |

Parallel with the Camp Commandander's office was that of the *Kommandant WFSt. (Wehrmacht Führungsstab)* headed by General Alfred Jodl and *Oberst* Walter Warlimont.

On August 26, 1941, Hitler travelled with Mussolini by air to the captured Russian fortress of Brest-Litowsk and at this time, the 1st Company of the Battalion secured the airfield where Hitler's aircraft had landed.

As the war progressed, units of the FBB were sent to the eastern front for combat training. These combat units were called *Kampfgruppe Nehring* after the head of the Heavy Weapons Company. They operated in the northern sector of the line and initially consisted of:

One Panzer Company under the command of *Oberleutnant* Rohrbeck,
One Anti-Tank Platoon of the Heavy Weapons Company,.
One Motorcycle Platoon of the 2nd (motorized) Company,
One Armored Reconnaissance Platoon of the 2nd (motorized)
    Company
One Anti-Aircraft Platoon,
One Signals Platoon,
One Medical Platoon
One Workshop Platoon

This unit left from the railroad station at Rastenberg on September 24, 1941 for a three week long combat training period. They arrived at the front just as the Russians were beginning their winter offensive and the Battalion became engaged in heavy combat against Soviet infantry and armor, returning to Rastenberg in October of 1941.

The "*Wolfsschanze*" was in a state of constant expansion during the war and 1944, massive concrete structures were completed because of the strong possibility of air attacks. Although both the Russians and Americans were aware of the position of the headquarters, no attack was ever made on the camp. When Hitler left the headquarters in November of 1944, engineer units of the army blew it up so that all that remains are piles of shattered rubble.

The *Führer-Begleit-Bataillon* was formed into the *Führer-Begleit-Regiment* in September of 1944 and in November of that year, enlarged into the *Führer-Begleit-Brigade* which consisted of:

I. *Panzergrenadier Btl Führer-Begleit-Brigade*
II. *Panzergrenadier Btl Führer-Begleit-Brigade*
*Sturmgeschütz Brigade 200*
Signals Company
Artillery Section FBB with three batteries
Reserve battalion

On January 26, the Brigade was increased to a Division.

This unit fought in the Ardennes battle in January of 1945 and was then transferred to the eastern front where it was encircled at Spremberg and destroyed.

# A note on sources:

Baur, Hans, *Hitler's Pilot,* London, 1958.

Boelcke, Willi, ed. *The Secret Conferences of Dr. Goebbels, 1939-43,* New York, 1970.

Bormann, Martin, *The Bormann Letters,* London, 1954

Bullock, Alan, *Hitler, A Study in Tyranny,* New York, 1964.

Heiber, Helmut, ed. *Hitlers Lagebesprechungen,* Stuttgart, 1962

Hoffmann, Peter, *Hitler's Personal Security,* London, 1979.

Hubatsch, Walther, *Hitlers Weisungen für die Kriegsführung 1939-1945,* Frankfurt am Main, 1962

von Lang, Jochen, *The Secretary,* New York, 1979

Lochner, Louis, ed. *The Goebbels Diaries, 1942-43,* New York, 1948

Maser, Werner, *Hitler, Legend, Myth and Reality,* New York, 1971.

Moseley, Leonard, *The Reich Marshal,* New York, 1974

Picker, Henry, ed. *Hitler's Secret Conversations, 1941-1944,* New York, 1953.

Raiber, Dr. Richard, "Guide to Hitler's Headquarters," *After the Battle* magazine, Special Edition Number 19, London, 1977.

Schramm, Percy, *Hitler: The Man and the Military Leader,* Chicago, 1971

Sündermann, Helmuth, *Deutsche Notizen, 1945-1965,* Leoni, 1966.

Spaeter, Helmuth, ed. *Die Geschchte des Panzerkorps Grossdeutschland,* Vols I, II, III, Duisburg, 1958

Tessin, Georg, *Verbände und Truppen der deutschen Wehrmacht und Waffen-SS 1939-1945,* Vol. 14, Osnabruck, 1980.

Warlimont, Walter, *Inside Hitler's Headquarters, 1939-45,* Novato CA 1964

*The Führerhauptquartier War Diaries* located in the German State Archives and the U.S. National Archives;

Various records dealing with the FBB and *Kampfgruppe* Möhnke located at the Hoover Institute.